"This volume should not be required reading, but required study for everyone offering care in America. The biggest complaint about care in the USA is that "nobody listens." Tom Balles' book lays out, in simple detail, the basic human habits that we lost in our addiction to technology. Care is about individuals caring for other individuals."
—Robert M. Duggan, MA, MAc (UK), Dipl Ac (NCCAOM), author of *Common Sense for the Healing Arts* and *Breaking the Iron Triangle: Reducing Health-Care Costs in Corporate America*

"*Becoming a Healing Presence* is simply elegant. Tom Balles calls all those who offer care to a high standard—to be present, with senses wide open. He offers uncomplicated practices for exploration, inviting us to sharpen our attention and deepen our awareness. Tom knows the rewards are great when we infuse our care for another with authenticity and compassion. The book serves head and heart and will transform the caring experience for both giver and receiver."
—Barbara Catlin, founder and director, Bigger Conversations, Columbia, Maryland

"The Sufi poet Rumi called us to "be a lamp, or a lifeboat, or a ladder." In this new good book, *Becoming a Healing Presence*, when Tom says, 'Please accept the gift of these words,' he is calling us to ways of being a lamp, a lifeboat, and a ladder for others. Thank you, Tom, for your guidance. I am in practice with you."
—Dianne Mary Connelly, PhD, MAc (UK) Dipl Ac (NCCAOM), author of *All Sickness is Home Sickness* and *Medicine Words: Language of Love for the Treatment Room of Life*

"Tom Balles' book, *Becoming a Healing Presence*, caught my attention immediately when he highlighted five human core needs: to be touched, understood, acknowledged, heard, and seen. This important book shows ways of interweaving these basic needs into patient communication and care, thereby creating a more effective healing presence."
—Fritz Frederick Smith, MD, founder of Zero Balancing®, author of *Inner Bridges* and *The Alchemy of Touch*

"*Becoming a Healing Presence* is an evocative and inspiring manual that is essential for anyone providing care. With a wealth of wisdom from his years of clinical experience, Tom encourages us to speak and live from the depths of our hearts. He clarifies and deepens the idea that our presence alone can have a healing effect on our selves and others. In an era when the relationship between patient and practitioner is too often mechanical, Tom's voice calls us to be authentic, present, and compassionate. In his new book, he gives us an invaluable roadmap to the experience of wholeness that is possible between any two human beings."
—David Mercier, LAc, author of *A Beautiful Medicine: A Radical Look at the Essence of Health and Healing,* Grand Winner 2013 Nautilus Book Award

"Tom Balles is a worthy guide to aid us to be ever learning, ever becoming the healing presence that, at our core, we always are."
—John G. Sullivan, PhD, author of *The Spiral of the Seasons: Welcoming the Gifts of Later Life* and *Living Large: Transformative Work at the Intersection of Ethics and Spirituality*

Becoming a *Healing* Presence

A Guide for Those Who Offer Care

Tom Balles

iUniverse

BECOMING A HEALING PRESENCE
A GUIDE FOR THOSE WHO OFFER CARE

Copyright © 2015 Tom Balles.

All rights reserved. No part of this book may be used or reproduced by any means, graphic, electronic, or mechanical, including photocopying, recording, taping or by any information storage retrieval system without the written permission of the publisher except in the case of brief quotations embodied in critical articles and reviews.

iUniverse books may be ordered through booksellers or by contacting:

iUniverse
1663 Liberty Drive
Bloomington, IN 47403
www.iuniverse.com
1-800-Authors (1-800-288-4677)

Because of the dynamic nature of the Internet, any web addresses or links contained in this book may have changed since publication and may no longer be valid. The views expressed in this work are solely those of the author and do not necessarily reflect the views of the publisher, and the publisher hereby disclaims any responsibility for them.

Any people depicted in stock imagery provided by Thinkstock are models, and such images are being used for illustrative purposes only.
Certain stock imagery © Thinkstock.

ISBN: 978-1-4917-6574-6 (sc)
ISBN: 978-1-4917-6575-3 (e)

Library of Congress Control Number: 2015905739

Print information available on the last page.

iUniverse rev. date: 04/22/2015

To my beautiful wife, Nancy, the love of my life

In their core, people want to be touched. Open your heart. Extend your hands. Offer the simple gifts of warmth, laughter, and lightness. Your vulnerability and tenderness will open the hearts of others. In your presence, they will know: here is someone I can trust.

In their core, people want to be understood. Be thoughtful in responding to others' concerns. Create common ground. In your presence, they will know: here is someone who seeks to understand me.

In their core, people want to be acknowledged. Honor your patients exactly as they are, for each is a unique human being. Discover that which is blessed and dear to them. Help them grieve for what has been lost. In your presence, they will know: I can be myself here.

In their core, people want to be heard. Sit still. Open your ears. Be willing to travel to the depths. Explore the unknown. In your presence, they will know: here is someone who listens.

In their core, people want to be seen. Open your eyes. Look beneath the surface. Create a shared vision and direction. In your presence, they will know what it is to see eye to eye.

Contents

With Gratitude ix

Introduction xi

Part One   Ways of Being 1
                Practice 2
                Be Present 4
                Maintain an Observer 7
                Choose Large Mind 10
                Remember to Breathe 12
                Open Your Senses 14
                Design and Shift Your Mood 16
                Offer Your Unique Medicine 18
                Make Room for Patients' Emotions 20
                Let Yourself Be Moved 23
                Bring Laughter and Joy 25
                Bear Witness 27
                Be at Ease with Ambivalence and Contradictions 29
                Honor Your Patients' Decisions 31
                Let Go 33
                Take Care of Yourself First 35

Part Two   Ways of Doing 37
                There's Nothing We Do by Ourselves 38
                Listen 40
                Help Patients Become Better Self-Observers 41
                Learn to Dance 43
                Use Touch 45

Encourage Those in Your Care to Be Beginners.................... 47
Support Patients in Their Learning.......................................51
Design Practices..53
Assist Nature in Doing What Only Nature Can Do..............55
Work in Mystery.. 57
Perform the Right Kind of Magic 59
Plant Seeds..61

Part Three Ways of Speaking... 63
Create Empowering Narratives.. 64
Have Conversations That Matter 67
Listen for Plastic Words... 69
Help Patients Acknowledge What Is So 71
Make Sure There's No "It" Out There 72
Listen for the Opening...74
Take Risks..76
Call Patients Back to Wholeness 78
When a Patient Doesn't Know 80
When You Don't Know... 82
Be as Good as Your Word 84
Make Clear Requests... 86
Hold Symptoms and Signs as Wise Teachers........................ 88
Go Beyond the Literal... 90
Stay until the End 92

Final Thoughts 95

Further Reading... 97

About the Author..101

With Gratitude

I'm grateful to the following people for their invaluable contributions in creating this book:

To my wife Nancy, as the first reader, thank you for offering both support and challenge to the words I had written.

To Mary Ellen Zorbaugh, Guy Hollyday, Allyson Jones, and Elise Hancock, your comments early on smoothed out innumerable rough edges in the text.

To Laura Mueller, thank you for seeing that I was writing to all who offer their care, not just professionals. Your vision expanded my vision; your words sharpened my words. Thank you for your edits and seeing what I did not.

To Tom Payne, for your patience and the striking cover created around your photograph of the magnolia blossom. You have such an eye for beauty.

To Kimberly West-Fox, senior publishing consultant at iUniverse, your reassuring words and presence made the difference in getting me back in the door for a second book.

To all my colleagues, students, and patients over the last thirty years, you've been my teachers, and these pages contain the lessons I've learned from you. I'm grateful that I'm now able to share your wisdom with a larger audience.

Introduction

During the thirty years I've been an acupuncturist, the delivery of health care has gone through enormous changes. The insurance and managed-care industries have grown exponentially. Pharmaceuticals have become a first response to any complaint. Costly, high-tech medicine reflects our fascination with pathology and lack of attention to wellness.

In the midst of these changes, I wonder if we've developed a bit of amnesia. In offering our care, have we forgotten the capacity of human beings to help heal other human beings? Have we overlooked the need to cultivate ourselves as instruments of healing? Are we in danger of losing the healing power of the relationship between those giving and receiving care?

The large tribe of those who offer care is in need of some potent medicine. I offer these essays as constitutionals—powerful elixirs that remind us of the many healing capacities we possess and the great strength to be found in the healing relationship.

This tribe I'm referring to includes laypersons: those who begin offering care with little or no professional training. At some point in our lives, most of us will find ourselves in this role with someone close to us. This group includes the parents caring for a sick child, the adult child tending an aging parent, spouses and partners caring for each other, and the friend stepping up to assist an ailing companion.

The tribe also consists of volunteers: those who received a small amount of professional training in order to offer their care. Examples of volunteers include those gentle and courageous souls working in a variety of settings like hospice care, neonatal units, and emergency rooms.

The last group within the tribe is the health-care professionals. These include all those disciplined providers who go through years of rigorous training in order to offer care.

At first glance, it may seem these groups—laypersons, volunteers, and professionals—are too disparate a collection of people to make up a single tribe. Yet a powerful bond connects us all. Regardless of the level of care we offer, each of us has the ability to become a healing presence.

In my previous book, *Dancing with the Ten Thousand Things*, I explored what it meant to be a healing presence in a variety of domains—family life, friendships, the workplace, and community life. In this work, I focus specifically on what it means for those offering care to others in need. I again offer a working definition of what it is to be a healing presence. A healing presence cultivates distinct ways of being, doing, and speaking that serve life and the lives of those around them.

The essays are grouped into three parts around these distinctions. "Ways of Being" sheds light on how we manage our internal territories: being aware of what's happening inside ourselves while tending those in our care. "Ways of Doing" focuses our attention outward: being mindful of what we're doing and how we're doing our work. "Ways of Speaking" explores the power of words and using language as medicine.

This book preserves and expands upon an applied philosophy of healing that has evolved for the last forty years at Maryland University of Integrative Health (formerly the Traditional Acupuncture Institute and Tai Sophia Institute). John Sullivan, Julia Measures, Bob Duggan, Dianne Connelly, and Jack Daniel were some of the original weavers of this philosophy. On occasion, you might hear their voices and recognize some of their favorite sayings that have ended up in these pages. I'm not always able to remember who said what the very first time, so I offer instead a deep and collective bow to all my colleagues.

While teaching this applied philosophy over the last nineteen years, I've watched graduates go on to become a very distinct kind of caregiver. Whether entering the fields of acupuncture, herbal medicine, nutrition, health coaching, yoga therapy, or health promotion, these students are invited into a larger conversation about healing. Yes, they're being trained to be effective health-care professionals. They're also called to be a healing presence in all their relationships—around the dinner table with family, in friendships, in the workplace, and as members of their larger communities.

I've had the privilege of working with students as they explored this philosophy, pondered the principles, wrestled with the practices, and ultimately were transformed by them. Regardless of what form of health care they went on to offer, embodying this work produced lasting change in themselves and those they came to touch. I continue to observe in these students what John Sullivan describes as "less unnecessary suffering and greater possibilities" in the lives they share with others. I think you'll agree these are not small gifts.

You'll get the most from this material by taking your time with the essays. Read—do not just scan—the text. Although the essays are brief, each contains enough material to be a class in itself. The book as a whole could be used as the bones for a course syllabus.

Becoming a healing presence requires practice. The practices at the end of each essay are a critical factor in helping you embody the distinctions in the text. Over time, they'll become second nature to you. Please hold the practices not as prescriptions but as invitations to new ways of being, doing, and speaking. They'll provide you with fresh perspectives and revitalize how you care for others. A further discussion of what it means to be in practice will be found in the first essay of part one.

Regardless of the role you play in offering care, these essays and practices will deepen your relationships with those you tend. Beginning students in health care can share this work with classmates and faculty. For professionals struggling with burnout or compassion fatigue, these essays provide new possibilities of how to tend yourself and your patients. When finding yourself in the role of patient, you could even be so bold as to share this work with the person tending you!

In writing about those who receive our care, there's the challenge of what we call them. Currently popular words like clients, customers, and even guests are too generic for my tastes; they could describe participants in any kind of financial transaction. On the other hand, the roots of the word patient are *pati* and *patiens*: the one who suffers. This clearly describes the person receiving our care—even if it is a family member or friend. Since it's also a role each of us will find ourselves in at some point in our lives, I've chosen to primarily use that word throughout. I also employ phrases like "those we're tending" and "those in our care" as synonyms.

The danger with such frequent use of the word *patient* in the text is we might start to believe it describes a group of persons who are somehow separate or different from those offering care. Rather, when referring to patients, let's remember that we're also pointing to ourselves.

My words are not the first words on these matters and will certainly not be the last. Whether acting in the role of layperson, volunteer, or professional, rest assured there are enough common threads in these pages to provide substance for all. For decades, this applied philosophy of healing has helped

Tom Balles

thousands of students learn to stay strong inside and focused on what truly matters when offering care. I hope it does the same for you.

From the beginning times of the Traditional Acupuncture Institute, Bob Duggan has encouraged his patients, students, and colleagues to give this work away. For more than thirty years as an acupuncturist and nineteen years as an educator, it's been my joy and privilege to do just that. Please accept the gift of these words. Now they belong to you.

Part One

Ways of Being

Part one focuses our attention primarily inward, on what goes on inside our skin as we offer care. These essays encourage us to be fully human in our relationships with patients while remaining attentive and present to their concerns.

The demands of tending others give rise to many questions:

- How do we maintain our observing self on particularly challenging days?
- How do we recognize the unique gifts we possess in offering care?
- How do we respond when patients share their emotions?
- What if we don't agree with decisions that patients make?

The essays and practices in this section provide effective responses to these questions.

The standard for staying present in our dealings with those in our care must be high. It's a bit too easy on some days to sleepily carry out our tasks as one moment blurs into the next. How different it can be to respond to the unique concerns of each person we tend. The experience rewards both those giving and receiving care with the depth of human contact.

Authentic care and compassion are palpable; people feel them when they're present and know when they're missing. Let's take good care of ourselves as instruments of healing so patients receive the outstanding care they deserve.

Practice

My friend and teacher Jack Daniel tells this story. Many years ago, a woman called him to ask about receiving some acupuncture for her concerns. With a hint of pride, Jack informed the woman that he had been practicing acupuncture for about fifteen years. Somewhat aghast, the woman replied, "Well, when are you going to stop practicing and do it for real?"

This was clearly a bit of miscommunication, yet the exchange points to a key component of providing care: we are both practicing and doing it for real. The most skillful performers in any field are lifelong learners. They're the ones with enough humility to recognize there's always something more to learn. These masters continually hone their skills even after years of being in the field: focusing on what they don't do so well and practicing until they're good at it.

The applied philosophy of healing outlined in these pages rests on the notion of practice. It's through practice that care and compassion are transformed into effective action. It's through practice that words on a page sink into our flesh and blood. Our ways of being, doing, and speaking become transformed.

The essays in each section are followed by one or more practices. Some practices focus on our internal states, others on what we're doing externally, still others on how we use our words as medicine. The practices can be taken on for a day, even better for a week, and some for a lifetime.

Numerous strategies will keep you mindful of your caring practice throughout the day:

- Create prompts (Post-Its, smartphone alarms, etc.) to wake yourself up when you forget.
- Keep a log or journal and write a paragraph each day about how life showed up differently in you and around you.
- Invite classmates, colleagues, or others providing care to take on the practices with you. Meet regularly (virtually or in person) to discuss and share your progress. Doing so will greatly accelerate your learning.

Be diligent in applying yourself. Like a good scientist, put everything to the test. Jump in with both feet! By experiencing these practices for yourself, you'll gather all the evidence needed to measure their value.

I'm fond of saying that all the practices work great—except when they don't. At any time, if what you're doing isn't working with someone, then do something else. In the end, you'll be surprised to see how one simple action or statement on your part affects a positive and powerful change with your patient. Reducing unnecessary suffering and creating new possibilities in the lives you share with others is worthy work indeed.

Practices

- Identify one facet of offering care that you could improve upon. Take steps this week to increase your level of skill in that arena. Read more about it, watch a video, or find some time to practice with a partner. Be that lifelong learner!
- Leaf through this book, focusing on the practices at the end of each essay. Choose one practice to explore and take on that practice for the next week.

Be Present

The skills and techniques we develop in offering care are absolutely essential, but over time, they won't be enough. Applying our skills day in and day out without authentically connecting with others leaves everyone involved with a sense of something missing.

A key component in building this connection—this rapport with others—is the capacity to *be* present. We strive to maintain our attention primarily in the present tense. When it comes to this, most of us don't start off with the unflappable and supremely attentive mind of a Buddha. Fortunately, there are numerous ways we can support ourselves in staying present to another's concerns.

Whether tending a family member, friend, or patient in a clinical setting, it's important to know we're being assessed from the very first contact. The degree of attention we provide during this time leaves a lasting imprint. One of my wonderful acupuncture teachers, the late professor and doctor J. R. Worsley, shared one of his practices for staying attentive. Placing his hand on the doorknob before entering a treatment room was his wake-up call: time to set aside any personal concerns and shift his full attention to the person needing care.

If meeting a person for the first time, shake the person's hand and extend the same social graces you'd normally demonstrate when meeting someone new. Greet anyone else accompanying them. Make eye contact. Find out what name they like to be called and use it. By employing these basic social skills, we're building our physical presence. Even before offering any care, we're "touching" the person through our words, eyes, and being. Consciously and unconsciously, the patient begins to register how it feels to be tended by us.

Especially in our first contact, let's be aware of how we're being received. What is customary for us may not be customary for others. Personal, familial, and cultural differences can preclude us from connecting in our usual ways. Handshakes may not be appreciated. Extended eye contact may be considered an affront. In some religious traditions, physical touch with members of the opposite sex isn't allowed outside of a medical exam or procedure. If we sense that a patient is hesitating in response to our actions, it's time to ask what their customs allow. More often than not, we can trust that if we've crossed a boundary, the person receiving care will let us know. The simple words "I'm sorry" are usually sufficient to restore the connection.

In the first and subsequent visits, we'll often spend time sitting and listening. This means sitting *with* someone, not looming over them as if poised to run out the door! Keeping ourselves in a comfortable seated posture makes it easier to stay present. Feet on the floor, weight above the sit bones, back supported, and breathing from the belly helps us focus on the other and not be distracted by any stresses or strains in our own bodies.

For those who see numerous patients during the day, these steps surprisingly save time, not the reverse. Taking the time at the beginning to establish a connection and build rapport increases the sense of partnership in the healing relationship.

Carving out quiet moments for any subsequent phone calls allows us to give the caller our full attention without being distracted. This seems like common sense, yes? Yet I remember a particular new patient arriving at my door. The woman was upset with a recent call from her doctor. He had called to inform her she had ovarian cancer while making his way home through rush-hour traffic. Making calls while driving, returning e-mails, or finishing charts are great examples of how not to be present.

Everything our patients see, hear, and feel affects their experiences. For that reason, our manner of dress and the physical space we work in also need to be a focus of our attention. These should reflect the same qualities—neat, clean, organized, and comfortable.

For many years, I've worked alongside colleagues in a private practice. We have no office staff, and each of us tends our own administrative needs. My practice is to arrive early and take a few moments to make sure the physical space is up to snuff. Most likely, it's the Virgo in me, and the simple stuff does make a difference in people's perceptions. I straighten out the magazines, clean the surface of the reception desk, and make sure there are soap, toilet paper, and spray in the restroom. Knowing the external environment has been given attention allows me to focus even more on patients I'll see that day. For those offering care in a home setting, it takes only a few moments to freshen up the bedside area. Doing the dishes is optional!

All that we are, all that we do, and all that we say make a difference in the quality of the care we deliver. Our influence begins with the first contact. Bringing our full attention and presence to bear right from the start powerfully conveys our deep care and compassion.

Practices

- Within the first five minutes of your visit, write down the eye color of the person you're tending. Making regular eye contact builds rapport and demonstrates that you're being attentive.
- Once you know what someone prefers to be called, use that name. Do so particularly when you want him or her to focus on what you're going to say next.
- Practice moving your seat closer to and farther away from patients and watch how they respond. Sit the distance (and direction) away that provides them the most comfort.

Maintain an Observer

The challenges we face when offering care stir up a variety of thoughts, feelings, and responses. Tending to the ill family member who's particularly cranky today, having a disagreement with a fellow volunteer, or getting behind schedule with patient visits are just a few examples of what can put us in reactive mode.

Looking closely, we observe that our thoughts often travel down the same well-worn pathways. Our emotional responses become habits, and our negative moods are like friends we've known for years. Unwittingly, we bring them into our interactions with those in our care.

Most likely, these practiced ways of responding served us in some way in the past. Over time, they became our default mode, a fallback stance, and sometimes our prison. We end up on automatic pilot, reacting to the daily ups and downs in our work.

In contrast, *maintaining our observer means recognizing we have a choice* about how we respond to the events of the day.

Let's take an example of the frustration we feel with those who dismiss our suggestions. Maybe we're tending a family member who resists taking prescribed medications. Maybe we're tending a patient unwilling to make the dietary change recommended by the nutritionist or one not doing the stretches outlined by the physical therapist.

Maintaining our observer means shifting from our automatic responses to seeing we have a choice about how to respond. When we move from habitual reactions to having our observer in place, the internal conversation shifts like this:

"I'm frustrated."

to

"I accept that I'm feeling frustrated."

to

"I'm choosing to feel frustrated."

In this context, the phrase "upset is optional" makes total sense. Our frustration is not likely to help us smooth out the relationship with those who dismiss important suggestions for their care. Neither is it likely to help with the cranky family member, resolve the disagreement with a fellow volunteer, or get us back on schedule with patient visits. In fact, when our observer isn't in place, we'll usually end up adding fuel to the fire.

This powerful practice can be utilized to shift many of our responses to situations that arise around us. Practice with the boilerplate below and plug in the following words in lieu of the letter *x*: upset, angry, resentful, lonely, anxious, depressed, sad, frightened, guilty, etc. See what shifts inside you.

"I'm x."

to

"I accept that I'm feeling x."

to

"I'm choosing to feel x."

Giving name to the phenomenon that's taking place inside us—and acknowledging we have a choice—shifts our perspective. We move from default mode and habitual responses to the choice point. We can choose to think, feel, speak, and respond differently than we may have in the past. With choice, we have freedom, and freedom gives us power.

observer

to

choice

to

freedom

to

power

Part two explores how to assist patients in maintaining their observers. To do so requires that we know how to do the same. Talking the talk won't cut it. We'll need to walk the walk as well.

Practices

- When you find yourself in reactive mode, actually write down and complete the process described above. For example:

    - "I'm resentful."
    - "I accept that I feel resentful."
    - "I'm choosing to feel resentful."

Becoming a Healing Presence

Seeing words on paper will help you recognize you have a choice about your response. In the same vein, say the same phrases to yourself. Better yet, say them out loud. Hearing the choice you've been making frees you to make another choice.

- When you become aware you're in a not-so-helpful mood or state, say to yourself, "How fascinating!" This phrase is almost magical in its ability to help us detach a bit, be more curious, and find out more about what's taking place inside.
- Identify three other actions you could take in response to a challenging situation.
- Choose a response that moves life forward for you and those in your care.

Tom Balles

Choose Large Mind

Losing our observer, we shift back into our practiced ways of being, doing, and speaking. In the previous essay, I referred to this as our fallback stance or default mode. We can also call this our *small mind*.

When we're in reaction, having lost our observer and our choice about how we might respond in a situation, we revert to a younger, more immature part of ourselves. These small-minded responses tend to increase our own angst as well as that of others around us. In contrast, our *large-minded* responses reflect the elder, the more mature, and wiser person who also resides in us.

The chart below contrasts how life shows up when we're in small mind or large mind. Note which mind you think produces more upset and breakdowns:

When in small mind, we …	**When in large mind, we …**
tend to be closed, hard-hearted, exclusive	tend to be open, warmhearted, inclusive
speak about faults, shortcomings	speak about strengths and gifts
tend to see in black and white (either/or)	are at ease with contradictions and ambiguity (both/and)
are oppositional	are cooperative
think in terms of obstacles, barriers	think in terms of possibilities and opportunities
see problems "out there"	examine our own choices, responses, and attitudes
are quick to blame, justify, and defend	are accountable and responsible
give power away	retain and use power
create separation and isolation	create connection and partnership
create false hopes, talk a good game	create clear expectations, embody humane conduct
are imprisoned	are free to choose
are asleep	are awake
suffer more	suffer less

It's not hard to recognize the signs of being in small mind: we cut ourselves off, close down, blame others, and suffer like crazy. Everyone around us, including those in our care, feels the ripples of the state we're in.

The first step in shifting to large mind is recognizing and accepting we're in small mind. The second step is to imagine what operating from large mind would look like and take steps to manifest it. Acknowledge how we're responding to the situation, choose another response, and jump back into the process.

Throughout the day, we move back and forth between small mind and large mind. One mind is not "better" than another. The difference is that responding from large mind reduces the amount of surplus suffering in and around us.

Regaining our observer takes practice. The good news is that it always brings us back to the choice point. From that place, we can, as my esteemed colleague John Sullivan likes to say, "Choose large mind!"

Practices

- As a way to practice being open, warmhearted, and inclusive, take steps during the day to extend yourself to those around you. Introduce yourself to someone new. Find a new way to connect with patients, coworkers, and colleagues.
- When you find yourself in opposition to what's taking place, take a step that reflects cooperation on your part.
- When wanting to blame others, justify your actions, or defend yourself, answer this question: "What part have I contributed to this situation coming about?" Translate your thinking into a new action you can take in the situation.

Remember to Breathe

What if I told you I had a device with which you could get your observer back in under a minute? Wouldn't this really come in handy on those days when it seems like everyone—yourself, your patient, others around you—is frantic or in a bad mood?

Let me tell you a little bit more to see if I can make a sale here. First, this device would be available to you twenty-four hours a day, seven days a week. It's totally portable. You can take it to work, the gym, the beach, and even through airport security. You can obtain this device without any start-up or activation fees. There's no annual contract to sign, and it even comes with a lifetime guarantee!

A pretty good product, eh? Just think how much less stress and tension you'd have if you owned it. Now, how much would you be willing to pay for this device—$50, $500, $1,000, or more?

The good news is that you don't need to purchase this device. You already possess it, and if you haven't already guessed, it is your breath. I consider the conscious use of our breath to be the fastest and most effective way to regain our observer.

Our breath naturally begins to slow down when we bring our attention to it. Slowing down the breath, especially with longer exhales, initiates the parasympathetic or relaxation response. We quickly return to the choice point. There we can take a moment to choose a more positive way of responding to the situation at hand.

I've noticed that on very busy days, I breathe rapidly in comparison to the amount of physical activity in which I'm engaged. It reminds me of the panting I do when jogging—shorter inhalations and longer exhalations, with my mouth slightly open. When stressed or moving fast at work, I sometimes actually amplify the panting and pretend like I'm jogging, letting the exhalation be longer than the inhalation. Surprisingly, and very quickly, my breath slows down.

What we often label as stress or anxiety is actually the body trying to keep up with the rapid pace of stimulation. So on those frantic days when it feels like we're "running" all day long, allowing ourselves to consciously breathe will serve us well. Our breath acts as a powerful antidote; making it less likely we'll be infected by any negative moods swirling around us.

Practices

- Place a written reminder or Post-It note on your computer or desk where you can easily see it. The reminder can be a simple one like, "How am I breathing?"
- If seeing more than one patient in the day, take at least three slow, deep, belly breaths between each session.
- Next time you are racing around to keep up, practice the panting style of breathing. Note how your breathing (and your mood) changes by doing so.

Tom Balles

Open Your Senses

Our ancestors had only their senses to go by. They looked, listened, smelled, tasted, and touched in order to gather information about those who were ill. Becoming skillful in offering care today still requires that we do the same: opening our senses and directing them both inward and outward.

Opening our senses *inward* means having an awareness of what's happening inside our skin. It means to look, listen, and feel for what's moving and changing inside us in the presence of those for whom we care. In healing relationships, both parties are touched, moved, and influenced by each other. During the course of any day, we can observe our feelings and moods changing, memories getting stirred, and stories and beliefs being challenged. Continuing to sense our bodies in real time helps sort out what belongs to patients and what belongs to us.

Opening our senses *outward* means being aware of what's showing up for those in our care. We look, listen, and feel for how life is moving uniquely through them. In every moment, patients offer up clues that reveal what's happening inside. Our challenge is to stay attentive and receptive so any stories we're creating about them are grounded in sensory phenomena.

By opening our senses outward, we also learn how we're being received. Is the person in our care looking away, crossing his or her arms or legs, or turning away from us? If so, it is time to check in to make sure he or she is still connected to what's going on and understanding what's being said.

We face a paradox here. Whatever the level of care we're offering, much of our learning came from teachers, books, and online resources. Yet in some ways, there was little these resources could teach us. None of the people in our care can be found in any text. They don't completely match any model, theory, or diagnostic category, and they are not an algorithm, percentage, or statistic. None of the people we tend to actually exist in a measurement world. They live in the flesh and can only be discovered by coming back to our senses.

When an attentive family member sees a change in pallor, the volunteer hears a change in the voice, or the professional feels more or less strength in the handshake, each of them knows that change is taking place. The knowing that arises from hearts and bellies—our intuitions and instincts—begins by opening the senses.

I'm not advocating we do away with any of the newer methods we have to gather information about those in our care. I am saying we can still learn from our ancestors. Opening our senses provides a trustworthy way of knowing and contributes to an unsurpassed quality of care.

Practices

- In the first five minutes of being with the person you're tending, take note of what you see, hear, smell, or feel. Can you detect any changes in pallor, voice tone, grip, handshake, or odors in the room? Write down any intuitions or instincts you have about them. How will this information now guide you in your care?
- Consciously exposing yourself to a variety of sensory stimulation is a powerful way to sharpen your sensory skills. It also gives you a break from your role in offering care. Explore the following activities, preferably with another, and write down all that comes to you via your senses:

    - Give your eyes something different to see—take a drive, watch a movie, read a book, look at art, go to a museum, head into the city, or go out in nature—to a beach, forest, or lake.
    - Give your ears something different to hear—listen to different music, surround yourself with different voices, or go out and listen to the sounds of nature.
    - Give your nose something different to smell—use essential oils or perfumes, visit a bakery, or go out in nature. (Do you see a pattern here with being in nature?)
    - Give your taste buds something different to taste—change your diet for a day, eat something new or different, or find something you can taste in nature.
    - Give your hands/skin something different to touch—take a warm bath, jump into a hot tub, get a massage, or touch things in nature.

Design and Shift Your Mood

Our emotions can be likened to changing weather patterns in a given day. They rise and fall like the temperature, come and go like the sun and clouds, and pick up speed and die down again just like the wind.

Moods are more like the seasons. They tend to settle in, linger for longer periods of time, and have a more profound affect on our state of mind, actions, bodies, and conversations.

Moods are more contagious than the common cold! Regardless of whether we label them positive or negative, they can immediately infect everyone around us—spouses or partners, family members, friends, colleagues, and certainly those in our care. We take great care to help our patients avoid pathogens and heal from infections. Let's take equal care to not infect them with moods that don't serve their healing.

We're always in some kind of mood or another. The good news is that we have the ability to not only shift our negative moods but also design positive moods that forward our own lives and the lives of those around us. Taking on the practices below helps us more quickly identify the mood we're in and shift it, if necessary, to one that keeps life moving in a positive direction.

Practices

- Design a positive mood. Before your feet hit the ground in the morning, make a declaration: choose a positive mood, such as joyful, peaceful, focused, calm, or thoughtful. Throughout the day, observe what moves you out of the mood and how you bring yourself back to your declared mood.
- Be aware of when you are in a negative mood and give it a name: frustrated, resentful, or jealous. Doing so moves you back to the choice point: you can stay in that mood or move out of it. Remember, choice gives you freedom, and freedom gives you power.
- Different moods live in different bodies. Change your posture. Walk differently: faster or slower. Put on some music and dance. Put your body in different positions (stretching, yoga, Tai Chi). Do some kind of exercise.

- Give yourself new challenges. Take some common occurrences and do them differently: drive another route to work, use your non-dominant hand for a day, vary your routine around household tasks (brushing your teeth differently), or enlist a friend or partner to do something with you that you'd normally do by yourself.

Tom Balles

Offer Your Unique Medicine

In many tribal cultures, the elders closely watch the young children as they grow up. When it comes time for the boy to become a man or the girl to become a woman, an initiation ceremony is held. The elders often give the youths new names that reflect the singular gifts the youths possess that are essential to the life of the tribe.

What would it be like for all those who offer care to pass through a similar ritual? What could be more powerful than to have everyone who tends others know the unique medicine they carry in their beings?

First at Tai Sophia, and now at Maryland University of Integrative Health, Dianne Connelly guides students through this ritual. A student will first hold out his or her arms in front as if holding a basket. Classmates then offer words to the student, reflecting how life shows up in the student's presence. A fellow student acts as scribe and writes the words down on paper.

The offered words are not meant to identify the student's skills, talents, or goals. It's not about what one likes or appreciates about the student, and does not imply a decision or commitment on the part of the student. The words reveal what Dianne calls a student's promise: what others know of life *through* that student, what comes to life in his or her presence. It's what we can count on from the student when he or she walks into a room. The promise reflects those inherent qualities of being that show up, no matter what. Most likely, these qualities were present since the person was born.

The offerings made to the student sound like this: "Mark, in your presence, I know life as great laughter and joy." "Mary, in your presence, I know life as quiet strength and possibilities." "Emily, in your presence, I know life as a calm stream of compassion."

The student sits with all the gathered words for days or weeks until he or she has edited and shaped them into a promise. A common, powerful form of the promise would read like this:

For the sake of all beings I, (insert your name), promise that wherever I am, no matter what, in my presence, life will show as (insert qualities).

One knows his or her promise rings true when others reply with a resounding "*Yes!*"

Guess what happens when you know how life shows up in your presence? Your medicine gets stronger. Whether you deliver your medicine via a foot massage at bedside or through a scalpel in the surgical suite, you come to know that no one possesses the same gifts you possess. No one offers what you have to offer. You're an original; your medicine is unique in the world.

Practices

- In the absence of a formal ritual, you can still hold out your basket. Inquire of others what they know of life *through* you, what they know of life in your presence. Take some days to sit with the words offered to you. Be creative and have fun shaping the words into your promise. Speak your promise back to them and listen for the booming "*Yes!*"
- Consciously practice delivering one particular gift to your patient(s) today. Take a particular quality of being and amplify it beyond what you might normally exhibit. Start with ones that come easily for you. For example, if you tend to be funny, see if you can get a laugh today from your patient(s), no matter the circumstances. Keep stretching each day by picking qualities you're less practiced at: offering understanding, inspiration, motivation, direction, etc. Observe how those in your care act in response.

Make Room for Patients' Emotions

This spring, a woman I hadn't seen in several years returned for some acupuncture treatments. Previously, she'd had her hip replaced. After telling her surgeon for more than a year that she had hip pain, he finally told her that her replacement would need to be replaced due to a structural defect (one he had suspected for some time). She spent much of the first session with me sharing the many emotions swirling inside her.

Primarily, she was furious that her doctor had suspected the cause of her pain and hadn't shared his suspicions for months. Her fury was just the tip of the emotional iceberg. She was relieved the cause of her pain had been finally uncovered, and she wasn't crazy. She was worried about the upcoming surgery, sad that her relationship with her surgeon had dissolved, and afraid of how she would fare with a second hip replacement. Over the next few sessions, we worked together to create a more positive emotional state in preparation for her next surgery, which another surgeon would perform.

Negative changes in the states of a person's health give rise to a variety of emotional responses in those we tend. Navigating this emotional territory can be challenging for both those giving and receiving care. There are several principles we can employ to keep us on solid ground:

It's rare for just one emotion to get stirred up during this time.

In exploring people's emotional responses, we're sometimes guilty, like the ambitious attorney, of "leading the witness." A statement like, "You must feel really sad about this," or a question like, "Doesn't this make you angry?" presupposes a singular emotional response and may mislead those we're tending into thinking they should feel one particular way.

There's no need to be reductionist here. Especially with abrupt or serious changes to one's health, it is better to expect and make room for multiple emotions to be expressed. Anger, frustration, relief, worry, sadness, and fear are among the many emotions that might arise at different times in the process. Asking about what emotions (plural) they're experiencing opens the door for the person to share a variety of feelings that may be present.

Once spoken, we can trust that speaking about one's emotions is healing in itself. We can rein in the tendency in the moment to "fix" the person, smooth over the emotions, or somehow make it all better. Simply acknowledging what they're feeling makes for good medicine, along with the reassuring reminder that with care and tending the emotional ride will smooth out over time.

In these times of change, patients tend to move more quickly from one emotional state to another.

During one visit, a patient may be angry and frustrated with his or her new situation and equally sad or grieving at the next. Two common phrases I hear are, "I'm overwhelmed with emotions," and "I don't know what I'm feeling." My ears perk up when I hear these phrases because they alert me to the possibility that my patient is experiencing rapid emotional shifts.

These roller-coaster rides come quite unexpectedly and can be quite disturbing to someone who is already dealing with daily discomfort and pain. Patients feel relief upon hearing that their experiences, although unpleasant, still fall within the norm.

When facing serious health challenges, a lack of emotional responses may be a red flag.

While offering care, we expect some emotional responses to a negative change in people's health and well-being: impatience with this new state of affairs, concern about what may be lost, or fear for how they will fare in the future. Some form of numbness, shock, denial, and disbelief are quite normal at the outset. However, consistently denying or glossing over any emotions may point to a need for professional counseling.

Abrupt or substantial changes to one's health naturally ripple through all levels of one's being: body, mind, emotions, and spirit. Taking the time to inquire about our patients' emotional responses helps them identify and stay in touch with these powerful movements. The time is well spent; it will contribute to successful outcomes for those in our care.

Practices

- In inquiring of those in your care how they're feeling, a common response is to describe one emotion. Take the step of asking the simple question, "What else are you feeling?"

- The other common responses to inquiries about patients' feelings include, "I don't know how I'm feeling," or "I'm overwhelmed at times." Practice being quiet for a moment and giving additional time and space for the person to go deeper and access what is present for him or her.

Let Yourself Be Moved

Those in our care are not the only ones who experience powerful emotional responses to their situations. Years ago, I was performing an intake with a new patient. I began the physical exam by reading the energetic pulses along the radial artery near her wrist. I felt some rough flesh beneath my fingers, and my chest suddenly got tight. Tears came to my eyes. Looking down, I saw the parallel scars from previous episodes of cutting herself that had gone unmentioned up to that point. I paused for a moment, took a few breaths to gather myself, and began a conversation about her experiences with cutting.

We're not required to give up being human when offering care. That morning in San Francisco, my tears took me by surprise, yet they were by no means the last tears I've ever shed in my treatment room. Patients sometimes bring very painful stories about their past or present circumstances. How can we not feel anger at injustices they may have experienced, be moved to tears of sadness for what they've lost, and share some fear about how they will get through this?

We face several challenges in these moments. First, it's critical to be aware of what's rising up in us in the presence of another's story. Mirror neurons in our brain may have us experiencing feelings similar to our patients, but we need to call our observer present. This is not about us.

Wanting to settle down inside, I have at times asked my patient to sit quietly for a bit. Taking some breaths helps a lot! Being vulnerable in this way does not diminish or take away from the conversation at hand. Instead, I've found that those I'm tending are relieved to know they have a real live human being tending them.

Being moved while offering care presents a second challenge: to not conspire with those whom we tend. The list of characters a patient might blame for his or her circumstances could be a long one indeed—a physician who doesn't listen, an incompetent surgeon, a lemon of a body, a less-than-perfect parent, child, spouse, partner, or boss, poor working conditions, or the uncaring Big Pharma that is out to get us all. Their stories touch our stories; their hearts touch our hearts. How easy it can be to join them in demonizing someone or something else for what's happening.

Simply acknowledging their feelings goes a long way. There is no need to jump into the waters of blame with them. Take a moment to regain your observer. Stand on the boat, throw them a life preserver, and pull them back on board.

Practices

- Knowing whom you tend to blame for painful circumstances in your life increases awareness of when you might conspire with those whom you tend. Make a list of those you're inclined to demonize. Keep the list handy. Seeing it in black and white will decrease the number of times you jump in the waters of blame with patients.
- Write down and practice speaking some verbal responses for those times when patients enter into a blame conversation. As a way to begin, find several ways to complete each of the following sentences:

    - "I understand you're angry with your doctor and …"
    - "I'm sorry to hear that your surgery didn't work out the way you planned and …"
    - "It sounds like you've really frustrated with your medications and …"

Bring Laughter and Joy

By the time I left San Francisco in 1995, more than ten thousand people had died from AIDS in the City and County of San Francisco alone.

It felt like the sun had gone behind the clouds and a pall had swept over the city; 25 percent of my acupuncture practice consisted of men who were HIV positive or had full-blown AIDS. Their lab reports often reflected a CD4+ T cell count of zero. On paper at least, they had no immune systems left.

Together, we didn't have the power to lift the pall. What we could do was create some sunlight in the treatment room, and we did so with laughter. There were many easy targets: the unending antics of the board of supervisors, the daytime and nighttime TV soap operas, and the public foibles of the rich and famous. There was much raucous laughter, and I remember leaving some sessions with tears in my eyes.

My time with these men was a powerful reminder that laughter is good for the soul. In addition to their own fragile health, many of them had already been to dozens of funerals and memorial services for friends and colleagues. Living in the middle of very dark times, they were craving a return of the sun: hungry for some warmth, laughter, and the lightness of being.

Many of our patients are also experiencing dark times; facing chronic illness, receiving a new diagnosis, or a return of an old one. In tending them, let's not forget to offer our warmth and spark some laughter. Your first reaction might be that you don't consider yourself to be very funny. At one time my colleague, Allyson Jones, said the same thing about herself. For the sake of her patients she practiced learning how to tell good jokes, and she now does so with aplomb. Lucky for those who get to see her!

Most of the men with HIV and AIDS who I tended in San Francisco lived well beyond their initial expectations. I certainly can't claim that offering laughter and joy in the treatment room extended their lives. I certainly can say that our time together brightened up their lives and my life as well. Maybe, just maybe, that's how we recognize good medicine—when both patient and caregiver are touched and moved.

Practices

- If you don't consider yourself to be very funny, take on the practice from Allyson Jones. Learn how to tell good jokes and keep a few fresh ones handy for your patients.
- Ask your patients about what they find funny or makes them laugh. Build some common ground with them in these areas. Feed the fire with your own offerings next time you see them.

Bear Witness

Years ago, I watched a television program in which a reporter asked the Dalai Lama about suffering. The Dalai Lama grabbed a fold of flesh on his forearm and said, "As long as there is this, there will be suffering."

Consciousness is attached to our physical bodies. Everyone we tend can identify some consistent aches and pains they're aware of in their bodies: lower back pain, skin conditions, digestive problems, difficulties with menses, joint pain, headaches, etc. Patients and those providing care work together to uncover what lifestyle factors contribute to the discomforts and then strive to keep them to a minimum.

If only it was that simple. We could hold everyone in our care as fully responsible and accountable for his and her own health. However, other factors make the picture much more complex. How much control does anyone have over

- genetic make-up, including race and gender;
- structural imperfections from birth;
- place of birth—country, geography, and climate;
- family of origin/extended family—parents, siblings, children, aunts/uncles;
- time/era of their birth—the accompanying technology, economic and political systems, social strata, means of transportation;
- upbringing—familial, religious, cultural, and educational traditions;
- autonomic functions of the body—respiration, circulation, lymph system, digestive system, neurological functions;
- people who appear in their lives—friends, neighbors, classmates, coworkers, colleagues, strangers;
- life experiences;
- accidents, injuries; or
- physical environment—air, water, soil, chemicals, toxins, noise levels?

Each of these impacts the health and wellness of our patients. Some factors they can influence to a degree; others they have less power to control. Given this context, can we still say that health is primarily one's personal responsibility?

Fortunate patients may ultimately benefit from successful surgery, appropriate medication, or a particular modality of care. We also need to remember that all their suffering will not end.

Whether we're tending a family member, volunteering, or working as a professional, it serves to have a conversation early on about the patient's expectations. Bob Duggan calls this "The Deal." What are the expected outcomes? How long will it take? Who is responsible for what in the healing relationship?

When offering care, we hold patients responsible for the factors they can control that affect their well-being. At the same time, let's not shield our eyes from any suffering that remains. Bearing witness means just that: to not look away from any of the pain that accompanies being human.

Practices

- If just beginning care of another, do have the conversation about The Deal as outlined above. Make sure all involved are clear about possible outcomes, how long it will take, and who will be doing what in the process.
- If already in a healing relationship, freshen up The Deal with your patient. Are you both on the same page in regard to what you're doing together? Clarify any areas where your expectations and the other's expectations differ.
- Take steps to free your patients from any unnecessary blaming of themselves for their state of affairs. Have a conversation to sort out those factors they can influence in regard to health—and those they cannot.

Be at Ease with Ambivalence and Contradictions

When facing important decisions in our lives, how many times have we had the experience of every cell in our body lining up and saying, *"Yes!"* to a choice we were about to make? I'm guessing that for most of us, it's quite a rare phenomenon.

It's the same for those in our care. Experiencing some new pain or discomfort—or receiving a new diagnosis—patients find themselves in unfamiliar territory. The way forward, the final destination, and the meaning of what's happening may not at all be clear. "Should I take the recommended medication or can I really change this with my diet?" "Must I do both chemotherapy and radiation?" "There's really no other option than replacing my knee?" "What's going to work best for my low-back pain: surgery, physical therapy, acupuncture, chiropractic care, or getting some great massages?"

In exploring possibilities of how to proceed, we're likely to hear phrases constructed like the following:

- My head says A, but my heart says B.
- One day I feel like A, the next day like I feel like B.
- One part of me wants to do A, but another part wants to do B.
- I could do A, but I probably should do B.
- Can I do A and B?
- I don't want to do either A or B, what about C?

Patients' thoughts collide with their feelings, instincts clash with intuitions, and their old stories conflict with what's so this time around. The resounding *"Yes"* shows up missing. Instead, they waver and vacillate.

Ambivalence, ambiguity, and contradictions are common stops in the healing journey. Our work does *not* include sorting all this out for those in our care. We watch, listen, inquire, support, and allow for the confusion that often precedes clarity. Their choices may not align with what would be our choices. What a great time to remember that it's their healing journey and not ours.

Practices

- Practice listening for the word *but*, which often points to the presence of ambivalence. Encourage your patients to insert the word *and* to see how that makes a difference in their thinking.
- When patients seem stuck in an either/or conversation, assist them in creating a third or even fourth option for how they might proceed. (Remember, doing nothing at this time is always an option.)

Honor Your Patients' Decisions

Those in our care don't always take the path we think is best. They refuse procedures and surgeries that could extend their lives. Medications to improve organ function or decrease pain are declined. Counseling or alternative modalities that might ease their suffering get turned away.

At the beginning of the healing journey, patients look to benefit from professional care and seek suggestions, solutions, and advice. They want the health-care professional to possess more expertise than they do, have more data about their concerns, have clinical experience with it, and skills in changing it for the better. The professional does the best job he or she can, acting as tour guide and laying out a map of the jungle. He or she describes territory that's quite familiar to them and very unfamiliar to the one they're tending. Once that information has been shared and treatment possibilities outlined, it's critical that the conversation shift.

Regardless of the role we're performing, now is the time for listening. Patients become the guides. The conversation moves from the present to the future and shifts from one of information and data to a conversation about possibilities. How will they proceed? What will they decide to do? Who will be involved in their care? Rarely is there only one way through the jungle. As tempting as it might be, we choose to refrain from telling those in our care what they need, must, or should do next.

We may never be made privy to—let alone understand—the reasons behind our patients' decisions. Ultimately, we're not there to make decisions for them. We bear witness and honor the choices they make, knowing they have the primary responsibility for determining the direction their lives will take.

Practices

- Practice shifting the conversation from the present to the future, from data and information to one of possibilities. Call forth your patient as guide by employing simple questions: "What do you think about all this?" "So, what's next?" "Given all this, how do you want to proceed?" Choose to listen without interruption.

- Find words and phrases that make explicit your support of those in your care, especially when their decisions are different than ones you would make.

    - "I support you in …"
    - "I respect your decision …"
    - "I understand …"
    - "I appreciate …"

Let Go

The activity of offering care contains an extraordinary amount of movement and change. The capacity to let go in a timely manner is critical for our well-being. Doing so increases our ability to be present to those in our care.

First and foremost is the letting go of patients themselves. Depending on our roles, we see patients over varying degrees of time. If working in an emergency room, for example, we may only see a patient one time. We wouldn't normally create a lasting bond in these circumstances. Others will see the same patient over a period of weeks, months, or even years. The bond often becomes stronger, and letting go becomes more challenging for both patient and the one offering care. The most emotionally demanding situations are those when patients pass away while in our care. These moments call for a good dose of self-care to ensure we keep moving forward with those requiring our attention.

Patients leave the care of professionals for a variety or reasons. For some, their concerns have been successfully addressed and the provider's services are no longer needed. Other patients move out of town. Some will seek second opinions and head in other directions. When we do know our time together is coming to an end, it's important to acknowledge that fact in a conversation with patients. Both parties are served by cleanly ending the relationship.

There are other external influences that demand we know how to let go. Patients' improving or worsening states of health may have them moving in and out of our direct care. For those volunteering or working in large institutional settings, the personnel around us can change with each shift. New policies and procedures seem to show up every week. Even our professions as a whole morph and change over the years, transforming into something we barely recognize.

Successfully adapting to the changing circumstances around us requires that we let go internally. Read each phrase below, prefacing it with the words, "I let go of my ..." Note along the way any changes in how you feel in your body:

- agenda
- desire to fix
- need to control
- resistance
- blaming others

- expectations
- plans
- struggles
- hopes

Whether it's life outside or inside that's moving and changing, there's no need to build a shrine to the past. To not let go and to carry around life as it used to be only contributes to burnout and compassion fatigue. Life rarely unfolds the way we would like it to, and our work with patients provides constant reminders of this truth.

The gift in letting go is that it makes room. It makes space for new life to come forth. We're called to be both hospice worker and midwife. We say a proper good-bye to life the way we knew it, and make room for the arrival of the next wave of movement, transformation, and change.

Practices

- At the beginning of each week, ask yourself, "What will it serve to let go of this week?" In taking steps to let go, you'll make room for life to show up differently.
- If you're struggling to let go of something, reach out to others. Ask them how they let go. Increase the number of ways you have available for setting down that which no longer serves.

Take Care of Yourself First

While boarding a plane, the flight attendant provides critical instructions: in case of a loss of cabin pressure, put your oxygen mask on first before helping others around you. Offering care requires that we do the same: tending and nourishing ourselves first so we can truly be of service to others.

The layperson learns just how quickly his or her routines can get turned upside down when providing care. Sleep and nap schedules go out the window, time for exercise disappears, important household tasks go unfinished, and socializing with others becomes a nonevent. On rare occasions, laypersons have even died from exhaustion while tending those in their care. One of the biggest challenges facing those offering care is how to adapt to the new circumstances while not jeopardizing their own health and well-being.

Those acting as volunteers also face a similar task. Given their existing family and work obligations, how many hours, shifts, or rotations can one offer in a given week? What times and days work best? How many patients can they really provide good care to, without sacrificing themselves?

Health-care professionals are just as susceptible to neglecting their own self-care. The long hours of patient care, endless paperwork, and the emotional demands of their craft can easily eat into the time they devote to themselves.

When we neglect our self-care, the likelihood of abusing our patients begins to increase. The simple factors—being tired, hungry, and overworked—contribute to this phenomenon. We owe it to those in our care to see this doesn't happen.

There is, however, another side to the coin. An equally important facet of self-care is to not take any abuse from patients. Yes, they may be in pain and experiencing high levels of discomfort, but it does not give them free rein to abuse those providing care. The rules of civility *do* apply, regardless of whether our patients have migraines, PMS, cancer, or PTSD. Becoming the lightning rod for all of our patients' anger, frustration, and resentment serves no one in the long run.

Generating a kind heart toward others begins by caring for our own. Self-care means tending to our own physical, emotional, mental, and spiritual needs on a regular basis. Doing so guarantees that those we tend receive the best of who we are and the gifts we have to offer.

Practices

- Design your own practice this week to increase your self-care. Make sure to get fresh air each day, cook a great meal for yourself, and set aside time for meditation, prayer, exercise, etc.
- Check to ensure that those in your care aren't using you as the lightning rod for all their frustrations and upsets. If that is the case, have a conversation in order to set proper boundaries around their behaviors.

Part Two

Ways of Doing

When taking on the responsibility of providing care, we learn any number of new skills and techniques. Whether it's helping a loved one recuperate at home, sitting bedside in hospice, or inserting IVs, we're educated in what we're to do in our distinct roles. Over time, we go beyond learning *what* to do and begin learning the *how*. How we go about doing what we do makes all the difference in the world to those receiving our care.

These essays and practices continue to explore a philosophy of healing that shapes how we tend those in our care. Whether it's learning to listen, helping patients become better self-observers, or planting seeds of future change, each exemplifies an approach that deeply honors the integrity of every individual we tend.

Even with our best efforts, all our patients' suffering isn't going to end. No matter how far along they are in their healing journeys, all life continues to hold some pain. Remembering this helps us tend what can be tended and learn to bear what remains.

Tom Balles

There's Nothing We Do by Ourselves

I make an offer to my new students. Removing a fresh hundred-dollar bill from my pocket, I announce that I'll give it to the first person that can identify one thing they do by themselves between birth and death. The one caveat is that everyone in the room needs to agree that the person's response is correct. (Spoiler alert: I still have my hundred-dollar bill.)

Common replies from the students include, "I think by myself ... I feel by myself ... I see, hear, breathe, sleep, go to the bathroom ... by myself." Other students inevitably jump into the fray and reveal the chinks in their classmates' thinking.

They remind each other how everything that becomes us comes from outside our skin. Oxygen comes from all the green growing things. Our food comes from the earth and most likely was grown, cleaned, packaged, delivered, and maybe even prepared by others. Water gets filtered, pumped, and piped to our homes by people we'll probably never meet. Without these ingredients, there would be no thinking, feeling, seeing, hearing, breathing, etc. There would be no human life. Add in our clothing, homes, offices, infrastructure, etc., and we clearly see our inescapable partnership with our fellow human beings and the earth. If you still think you deserve the hundred-dollar bill, run your idea by someone close to you. They'll let you know how you're off the mark!

What's the point for those who provide care? The point is to question the limiting and painful story that somehow we're distinct and separate individuals doing this work all on our own. This exercise offers a powerful reminder of the inherent interconnection and interdependence we have with all of life.

This philosophy applies to the role of caring family member, volunteer, or professional. All the knowledge we have about our work was learned from others. Every piece of technology we employ was invented, developed, and manufactured by others. Although it sometimes feels like it, we're not solo acts. The presence and labor of others supports, sustains, and surrounds all our efforts.

How often do we acknowledge this inside ourselves? There really has only ever been one team: you and everyone around you. The narrow emphasis on *I*, *me*, and *mine* in our efforts limits the many additional possibilities that show up when we choose to work in partnership with others.

Really, it's not a trick question. There's nothing we do by ourselves between birth and death, including tending those in our care.

Practices

- Offer at least one thank-you each day to those who assist you in your work. When giving acknowledgments, it helps to be specific. Let others know in one sentence how their actions aid you in your efforts.
- Begin to see the environment around you as one living system. Observe how all the parts are interconnected and influence each other. What parts of the system are thriving? Which parts are not? What might you provide so the system works more smoothly and everyone in it has more ease?
- Every day for a week, reflect on the question, "If everything I think I am comes from somewhere else, who am I really?" Notice what shifts in you while reflecting. How does it change the way you offer care?

Listen

The phrase *primary-care provider* has come to mean the health-care professional who oversees the care offered to a patient. Does anyone else find this phrase a bit odd? When did primary responsibility for patient care leave the hands of the patient? Are they not still their best primary-care providers?

When listening, what would it be like to hold the patient as a knowledgeable and equal partner in the conversation (the true expert in the room)? After all, who knows patients' histories better than themselves? Who better to provide the narrative of how they've come to this place? Who knows most intimately the physical, mental, emotional, and spiritual challenges they face in their lives? Who knows more about what kind of food, sleep patterns, exercise, work, and forms of enjoyment really serve them? Could we find any better guides to help them regain their health and well-being?

These simple acts of speaking and listening have been a key component of the healing ritual for millennia. In conversations with those we tend, it's absolutely critical to gather the facts. The real surprise is how little time it takes to inquire beyond the data. How does a patient feel about all of this? What does this mean to them? If nothing else, asking these two questions early on deepens the healing relationship.

Listening doesn't require a certificate, degree, or license. It's actually a gift, freely given to the one in our care. For some patients, the opportunity to be heard is priceless.

Practices

- Practice asking one question of your patients that takes the conversation deeper. How do they feel about what's going on? How are they coping? What does this mean to them?
- Support patients in being their own primary-care providers. Ask them, "If you were sitting in my seat, what helpful words and guidance would you offer this patient?"

Becoming a Healing Presence

Help Patients Become Better Self-Observers

We make many offerings to those in our care: the gifts of our time, attention, listening, compassion, and sometimes our love. There is another precious gift we have to offer. The Jewish philosopher Maimonides is credited with saying, "Give a man a fish, and you feed him for a day. Teach a man to fish, and you feed him for a lifetime." Helping those we tend become better self-observers may be the most precious gift we have to offer.

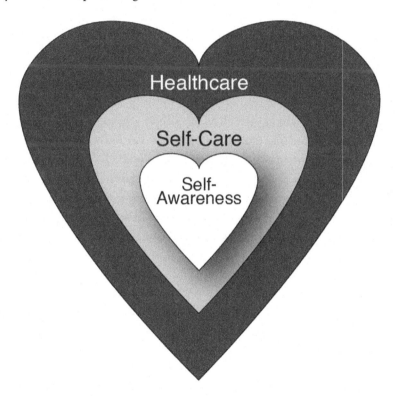

Self-awareness lies at the heart of self-care, and self-care lies at the heart of healthcare. The biggest rewards for patients in the healing relationship often show up when we ask them to observe for themselves what happens when they do, *x, y,* or *z*.

"What did you notice after skipping lunch?" "How did you feel the morning after staying up so late?" "Were you getting enough fluids before your headache began?" One doesn't need to be a health-care professional to pose these basic questions. Not surprisingly, feeling better often involves getting back to basics: eating nourishing foods, staying hydrated, getting sufficient rest and exercise, engaging in joyful activities, and socializing with others. It can take just a few reminders from us to reduce the symptoms and signs of distress.

For some patients, becoming aware of what takes place inside their bodies will take much time and practice. The process is well worth the effort, as those in our care will become more adept in managing their own care.

One effective tool is helping patients shift their language from abstractions to embodied phenomena. For example, someone might say, "I've been feeling really low this week." Truth be told, I have no idea what "feeling really low" means for this particular patient. I am, however, very curious to find out *how* he or she knows. Did the patient notice a heaviness or coldness in the chest or abdomen and decide to label it "feeling really low?" Has the patient become aware of self-critical thoughts popping up in his or her head all day long? Is the patient noticing changing behaviors: sleeping in more often, not eating as much, or not returning e-mails? It's much easier for both the patient and caregiver to tend embodied phenomena than to tend abstractions.

With perseverance, anyone can become a better self-observer. As their ability to do so increases, patients naturally assume greater responsibility for their own well-being. The wisdom from within the body reveals itself and produces great rewards for both patient and caregiver.

Practices

- Help each patient identify three or more early warning signs that reflect a negative trend in his or her health. (These might include getting more or less sleep, a change in appetite or energy level, frequency of headaches, changes in menses, condition of skin, etc.) Regularly inquiring about these markers helps those in your care become better self-observers.
- Put an extraordinarily powerful tool in your hands by asking the "how" question. Practice asking patients how they know they're stressed, exhausted, overwhelmed, tired, etc. Doing so shifts the conversation from one of abstractions to embodied phenomena, and it guides both of you in next steps that can be taken.

Learn to Dance

Partnering with those in our care is not unlike learning intricate dances. Some steps we're familiar with, but others may be quite foreign to us. Stumbling and fumbling or tripping and falling are not unusual. Learning to dance well together might require more than a few lessons for both partners.

Moving skillfully and gracefully across the dance floor means having the capacity to express a variety of ways of being, doing, and speaking. Each entry below contains two sides of qualities or capacities essential for being good dance partners. While reading the entries, note on which side of the equation your tendencies lie when you are tending others—where you're more practiced than not.

Sometimes it serves to …	*and*	sometimes it serves to …
speak		listen
lead		follow
be firm		be flexible
be direct		be indirect
teach		learn
be playful		be serious
give		receive
think		feel
take in		let go
accept		decline
be literal		be metaphorical
be a beginner		be a master

The personalities of those in our care are so varied and their circumstances so unique that it behooves us all to become better dance partners. Many more qualities and capacities are possible than those listed above—feel free to add to the list!

Practice

- After noting on which side of an equation you tend to reside, take steps to stretch yourself to the other side. If you speak a lot with patients, practice listening more. If you tend to lead, learn to follow. If you tend to be firm, what would becoming more flexible look like?

Use Touch

Some years ago, a cold that turned into a sinus infection drove me to the local urgent-care clinic to obtain an antibiotic. The physician entered the room, asked some questions, applied a tongue depressor, wrote a prescription, and left.

After she left, I realized she had never physically touched me. No handshake of introduction, no steadying of the head while looking at my throat, no palpation of lymph glands, and no reassuring touch on arm or shoulder; there was no touching whatsoever. Much showed up missing for me in that exchange.

More than any other means, physical touch expresses our willingness to be with another—no matter what. It's among the most powerful methods for healing living creatures. Touch succeeds where verbal communication falls short, and it is sometimes the only way to reach another. A gentle touch provides direct contact with the place that hurts, a gesture that begins the healing process.

Simply by being a spouse/partner, son/daughter, mother/father, or dear friend to others, we already offer many different kinds of touch. How hard can it be to deliver the same to those in our care? It takes no time at all to offer a firm, reassuring touch to an anxious patient. A playful pat to a frightened child's head quickly brings a smile of relief. A light and respectful touch affirms our empathy for a patient grieving a loss.

Clearly, in some clinical situations, physical touch may be impractical and inappropriate, if not illegal. And yes, some people do not like to be touched. For these reasons, I hold the opportunity to physically touch my patients as a true privilege.

The benefits of offering touch greatly outweigh the risks of being rejected. If patients don't appreciate your touch, rest assured, they will let you know. If you see them tense up, cross their arms or legs, or turn away, a simple apology will suffice.

Clearly, how we touch the patients we're tending goes beyond physical touch. The quality of our presence also influences them. In being still, we demonstrate the possibility of becoming calm. In being strong, patients find their strength. In being silent, they find their own words. In being patient, we give them time to do the same.

The words we use are a third form of how we touch patients. We employ language to teach, guide, encourage, inspire, support, and reassure. At times, we find it's necessary to use words like a scalpel, penetrating to the depth where the pain truly resides. How to use language as medicine will be explored in part three.

Touching others via physical touch, presence, and words are critical skills for us to possess. Healing begins by touching the place that hurts without causing more pain. Learning to do so requires us to practice. It also requires courage. So be it. Let's hold it as the gold standard for all our care.

Practices

- Increase the amount of physical touch you use until it becomes second nature. Expand the range of touch you incorporate: firm and reassuring, directive, playful, supportive, respectful, etc.
- Make it your goal to touch—and therefore positively influence—every person you tend via your physical touch, presence, and words.

Encourage Those in Your Care to Be Beginners

"My back has gone out again." "My blood pressure is spiking up." "I'm not sleeping so well." "I'm really getting more anxious." When hearing these words from those in our care, our first thought might be that the wheels are coming off the track or that something's out of balance.

Then again, maybe that's not it at all. Maybe it's just the opposite. Everything is quite all right. Life is on the move, and our patients are entering brand-new territory. Like Dorothy in the *Wizard of Oz*, they realize they're not in Kansas anymore.

Movement, transformation, and change are constants in life. More often than not, when we speak with patients, they're transitioning from one place to another, stepping into new territory that's quite unfamiliar. They don't yet feel competent, confident, or comfortable, and they face a steep learning curve. Symptoms and signs of discomfort begin to appear. We can offer potent medicine by helping those we're tending recognize they're beginners in this new territory.

What kinds of transitions might people be going through?

Being Beginners at Facing New Situations and Events

Patients find themselves needing to adapt to new situations and events regardless of whether they label them positive or negative. We can trust changes are coming when a patient's son or daughter is about to get married, a hoped-for promotion at work adds greater responsibilities, or a house is bought for the first time. At the negative end of the scale, changes will also come when the economy takes a downward turn and one loses savings, retirement funds, or a job. Getting injured in an accident or being a victim of a natural catastrophe—the list of new situations goes on and on. Maybe most importantly, patients will be beginners when adjusting to a new diagnosis: "You have diabetes ... asthma ... cancer ... you've had a stroke."

Being Beginners at Relationships That Shift and Change

Because we're such social beings, when our significant relationships change, we change. Maybe a long-time spouse or partner begins to pull back. A son or daughter becomes estranged. We fall head over heels in love. A good friend moves a long distance away. A wonderful boss at work departs, and chaos results. A loved one gets ill or passes away.

Being Beginners at Moving into New Stages of Their Lives

Childhood and adolescence are often accompanied by their own brand of pains and discomfort. Then come the increasing responsibilities of being spouse, partner, parent, and householder. The elder years can be a treacherous journey for some, filled with declining health and many unknowns. With a little luck, we become wise sages or crones, yet thoughts of mortality are not far away. Each of these stages requires adaptation on all our parts, including those in our care.

As much as we believe we're prepared for new situations, shifting relationships, or different stages of life, the embodied experience of them frequently comes as a surprise. Caught unawares, we're more deeply touched than we'd imagined. Surprised by our own responses, the nagging thought is that we *should* know how to be with these transitions, what to do about them, or what to say. Symptoms and signs of discomfort often begin to manifest on some level of our being.

The phrases below highlight some of the transitions outlined above. Recite the phrases out loud, beginning each phrase with the words: "My patient is a beginner at …" Notice if anyone in your care comes to mind.

- going off to school for the first time
- taking tests, failing tests
- experiencing puberty, becoming a teenager
- having a first boyfriend or girlfriend
- resolving conflicts
- breaking up with a first boyfriend or girlfriend
- exploring his or her sexuality
- having sex
- falling in love, falling out of love
- going off to college
- having a job, losing a job
- stopping smoking, drinking, or using recreational drugs
- exercising
- gaining weight, losing weight
- being married or in a committed relationship for the first time
- being a mother or father for the first time

- being a mother or father for the second or third time
- being married for ten, twenty, or thirty years
- being separated from a spouse or partner
- being divorced
- returning to school
- having a child die
- having a serious accident or chronic illness
- retiring
- taking care of their aging, ill, or dying parent
- having a parent die
- dying

When patients recognize where they're beginners, a new and compassionate light shines on their discomfort. For example, a woman I'd been treating began to be involved romantically with another woman. This was her first time being in an intimate relationship with a woman—not so for her new partner. My patient was losing sleep and eating less as she took baby steps into the relationship.

I took a risk by suggesting that she was a beginner at being in a relationship with a woman. I shared the metaphor that she was struggling to stay upright on a two-wheeler with training wheels still attached, while her new partner had already spent years tooling around on a racing bike! We both had a great laugh. Good medicine indeed.

Whether we're eight or eighty, each of us finds ourselves beginners: facing new situations or events, navigating changing relationships, or entering new phases of our lives. Symptoms and signs of discomfort often appear or reappear when faced with the new and unfamiliar.

By being beginners, patients let go of thinking they *should* know how to respond in these new situations. Greater ease shows up in their bodies and their physiology. Self-judgments begin to melt. Those tight back muscles begin to relax. Blood pressure drops a few points. Sleep improves. Anxiety decreases. Declaring one's self a beginner sets the stage for the learning that inevitably accompanies healing.

Practices

- Before each day begins, reflect on the patients you'll be seeing. What transitions are they facing? In what arenas are they beginners? Ask those you're tending how they're doing in these arenas—and how it's affecting their health.
- Especially with those who begin to exhibit an exacerbation of previously managed signs and symptoms, inquire about what's changing in their lives—for the better or worse. Assist them in exploring how and what they need to learn in these areas.

Support Patients in Their Learning

Being a beginner in any arena of life presumes there'll now be some learning that takes place. Yet the word *learning* stirs up a broad range of responses. For some patients, hearing the word provokes clammy palms, a churning belly, or beads of sweat on their brows. For others, the word moves them to the edges of their seats, eager to face new challenges.

Regardless of where our patients' reactions are on the scale, true healing will involve learning. Remember the patients described in the last essay? The one with a tight lower back may very well need to learn some new stretches. High blood pressure may suggest the practice of meditation. Difficulties with sleeping may signal a time to reexamine the bedtime ritual. The patient experiencing anxiety might benefit from learning some deep belly breathing.

I've observed four different kinds of challenges patients face in learning:

1. *I never learned how to do this.* Here patients are required to learn a new and essential skill. This could include anything from injecting the daily insulin shot, emptying the catheter bag, or learning proper wound care. We partner the patient as they experience the frustration that often accompanies learning something new.

2. *I learned how badly.* Whether we're laypersons, volunteers, or professionals, we support the patient in relearning some basic life skills. We offer them encouragement for the new exercise regime recommended by the physical therapist, provide support for necessary changes in diet and eating habits, and encourage them in setting proper boundaries with difficult family members.

3. *I learned how and forgot.* We can inquire about and call patients back to activities they've already taken on that served them well in the past. It could be time to get back to the daily walk outdoors, carrying a water bottle around again, or stepping away from the computer at night to get that extra hour of sleep.

4. *I learned how, and I don't know how in this situation.* We get to strategize and co-create practices with patients to fit their new circumstances. "I usually sleep okay, but now I'm waking up three times a night with the new twins." "How do I shower now that I

have this cast?" "How do I fit any kind of exercise in with all these doctor's appointments?"

Whether learning a new skill or relearning an old one, we trust that change will be involved. As the old Zen saying goes, "Fall down seven times, get up eight times." Our role is to steady patients who stumble and fall while facing the obstacles to change.

The authors of *Changing for Good* offer some useful distinctions for assisting patients who are ambivalent to learning and change.[1] Conversations with those in our care will differ depending on the stage they're in: pre-contemplation, contemplation, preparation, action, maintenance, and termination. Having the *right* conversation at the *right* time with those we're tending increases the chances of achieving successful outcomes.

Faced with learning and change, we often hear familiar phrases from patients: "This is too hard." "I'm not very good at this." "What can I do instead?" (Do you also recognize yourself here when you've been a patient?) We again offer the invitation to patients to be beginners in this new territory. The question here is not "What's wrong and how can we fix it?" The more helpful question is "What's possible here and how can we create it?"

My teacher, Dr. J. R. Worsley, used to say to students, "Educate, treat, and educate some more." The phrase reminds us of one of our central tasks. The Latin root of the word *educate* is *educare*: to call or bring forth, to lead out. Whether the patient is the nervous one with sweaty palms or the one on the edge of his or her seat with excitement, we assist them to call forth all their gifts and resources to face the challenges that lie ahead.

Practices

- Introduce the notion to those you tend that healing involves (and is even synonymous with) learning. What do they say they now need to learn in order to heal? How will they go about this learning? What barriers might show up? How will they respond to the barriers?
- Explore the distinct stages of change outlined in *Changing for Good*. Have the appropriate conversation with your patients that will serve them in their stages of change.

---

[1] James O. Prochaska, John C. Norcross, Carlo C. DiClemente, *Changing for Good*. New York: HarperCollins, 1994.

Design Practices

In offering care, the majority of us see patients on more than one occasion. The period of time we tend them ranges from a few days during a hospital stay to weeks, months, or years of supportive care. There's a tendency for some patients to put the knowledge of how they're doing—and what they need to do to heal—squarely in the hands of the experts. This applies to Western medical and alternative practitioners alike. One way to shift the patient's role from a passive one to an active one is by creating activities and practices together that patients carry out in the interim between visits.

The question of "What's possible and how can we create it?" now comes alive in the healing relationship. Working side by side with patients, the creative juices begin to flow as we create positive steps to place primary care back in our patients' hands.

Simple questions that prime the pump come from questions that good newspaper reporters asked in the past. They used the questions *who, what, when, where, how,* and *why* to flush out breaking news stories. We can employ these same questions in conversations with patients to help them identify what, exactly, is possible, and how they can create it for themselves:

- Who will help you with this? Who is on your team?
- What do you need to learn now?
- When will you begin?
- Where can you go to learn this?
- How will you go about learning this?
- Why do you need to learn this?

For example, we might ask the following questions of someone newly diagnosed with diabetes:

- Who is on your team? Who will partner with you in making the dietary changes that will support your well-being? Who will help you learn how to manage your medication?
- What do you need to learn now? Exploring new ways of eating, exercising, and learning how to administer medications certainly come to mind.
- When will you begin to make these changes? Today sounds like a good idea!

- How will you go about learning? The physician and nurse practitioner can help with managing medications, a nutritionist can guide you in dietary changes, and the Internet can provide access to a world full of healthy recipes.
- Why learn this? The quality of your health for the remainder of your life will depend on it.

No matter the roles we play or the settings in which we work, quality care includes motivating patients to change, supporting them when they stumble, and providing persistent guidance toward successful outcomes. The authors of *Motivational Interviewing in Health Care* provide an abundance of evidence-based tools for doing that.[2]

Healing and the learning that accompany it involve practice, time, and rigor. Designing steps and practices with patients dissolves any learned helplessness they may have acquired along the way. Those we're tending become full partners in the healing process, and primary responsibility for their well-being is placed back on their shoulders where it truly belongs.

Practice

- Set a goal of having all your patients leave their time with you committing to take a step in the interim to improve their well-being. Emphasizing that the commitment is to them (not to you) will strengthen their motivation.

---

[2] Stephen Rollnick, William R. Miller, Christopher C. Butler. *Motivational Interviewing in Health Care: Helping Patients Change Behavior.* New York: Guilford Press, 2008.

Assist Nature in Doing What Only Nature Can Do

These words were spoken by one of my acupuncture teachers, Dr. J. R. Worsley. Individually, we might prefer other words in lieu of nature: God, Allah, Spirit, presence, the universe, higher power, etc. Regardless of our preference, Dr. Worsley's words provide a useful way to understand our roles in the healing process.

Two things appear to be true about providing care to others. First, our patients' bodies know how to heal themselves. Second, they sometimes need help in doing so. For example, a physician sets a broken leg, casts it, and then lets it be for a period of time. When set properly, the leg and the patient are well on their way to healing. The same is true whether we're in the role of layperson, volunteer, or professional. We say what we say, do what we do, provide what we provide, and then we get out of the way. We're privileged assistants in a process that none of us fully understand.

Our presence as catalysts in the healing process is absolutely critical. Yet it's also a temporary role. We tend our patient as long as it serves them, and then we let them go.

Too often, we describe our more dramatic efforts as "saving" lives. To speak this way and frame our work in this fashion denies a crucial truth. All those in our care are going to die. We absolutely *extend* lives and improve the quality of lives, but declaring that we *save* lives allows both parties to hide from a shared destiny. All of our lives will come to an end.

Whether our relationships with patients last for minutes or decades, we share the tasks of assessing how we might serve, aligning ourselves with our patients' wisdom, and acting as catalysts through our offerings. Then we let nature, God, Spirit—all the higher powers—do the rest. Even at our very best, we're always servants to something greater than ourselves.

Practices

- Remind those in your care that their bodies know how to heal themselves. Notice how the conversations shift when you do so.

- Ask your patients what else (in addition to your tending) will be important in their healing. Responses will vary: prayer, time in nature, rest, meditation, exercise, or being with family or pets. Whatever the response, expand the conversation to outline the steps they'll take to include those components.

Work in Mystery

Besides higher powers being at work, there are other mysteries that surround us. Even though the journeys through illness and disease, pain and discomfort, accidents and surgeries are absolutely unique, we're taught there are markers we can always point to and count on to know that patients are healing.

Blood results and lab work improve, wounds heal, organ functions return—surely these are all good signs, yes? And yes, they are good signs. We're happy when we see them. But those who've provided care for a long time know better. They know the whole of our patients' journeys can't be graphed on a piece of paper. They know data never tells the full story.

Those with experience remember well the patient who recovered beautifully from one critical illness only to pass away from an "unrelated" illness the next year. They remember the one at death's door from the car crash, ready to give up the ghost, who goes on to make a full recovery. They remember the young ones, full of strength and promise who didn't make it, and the elders, given little chance, who did. They remember the one clean and sober for such a long time who makes one final plunge into the darkness. What we once held to be trustworthy markers of healing turn out to be less than reliable. The patients described in treatment records are not the same ones living in the flesh.

Depending on the outcomes, our patients' healing journeys come to be described in wildly different ways:

- being cursed
- bad luck
- a raw deal
- one's lot in life
- fate
- destiny
- karma
- good fortune
- gift
- blessing
- Providence
- God's will
- divine intervention
- a miracle

Who lives, who dies, who falters, or who thrives remains a mystery of the highest degree. Our participation absolutely influences our patients and the arc of their healing journeys. Unfortunately we tend to puff up with pride or burden ourselves with guilt, depending on the outcome. Both responses create unnecessary suffering.

A dose of humility serves here. Our efforts are only one part of the equation. It serves us well to let go of the need to understand and figure it all out. We can be peaceful, knowing our work is surrounded by mystery.

Practices

- Be gracious when those you tend thank you for your good care. Take in the acknowledgment by simply saying, "You're welcome."
- Write down and practice how you'd respond when patients see their situations in a negative light. Begin by creating several verbal responses to each of the following statements:

  - "Having this arthritis, it's just my lot in life."
  - "I got a raw deal with how that surgery turned out."
  - "It's just my luck to get cancer when everything else was going so well."

Perform the Right Kind of Magic

If we've been acting in the role of caregiver for any length of time, most likely we have seen a little bit of magic. It's not hard to remember the patients who end up doing extraordinarily well, in a very short period of time, with relatively little intervention on our part.

Even more magical is that even we don't know how it happened! Was it the excellent rapport created with the patient? Was it our superior skills in tending them? Was it the patient's motivation and commitment to getting well? Was it some combination of these factors, a bit of good luck, and more? As mentioned in the last essay, we hopefully accept our patient's thanks by humbly saying, "You're welcome" and living with the unsolved mystery.

Performing magic is one facet of our work that undoubtedly isn't found in any job description, yet it comes with the territory. And who among us doesn't like to be perceived as a magician?

Skillful magicians know that different kinds of healing have different relationships to time. Mending of the broken leg, healing of the stitched wound, completion of the postsurgical care take place *through* time and *over* time. No matter how good we are at providing care, the process won't be completed come the morning.

Other kinds of healing take place *out of* time. Occasionally, we witness the epiphany that changes everything, and it all takes place in a second. Patients with dangerously high blood pressure recognize in an instant that their future health lies in their own hands. The mother-to-be sees in a flash that now is the time to quit smoking. With one glance at each other, the bickering parents understand how their actions are hurting the children.

The shifting focus of health care and the accompanying rising costs seem to demand of us another kind of magic: that we learn to *speed up* time to accelerate the healing process. The best medications are certainly those that provide the fastest relief. The best surgical procedures and physical therapy get athletes back on the field in record time. The best psychological care should require only a few sessions to unravel conditions that have been in place for decades. Speed has become the new measure of the good: the new morality.

In our great hurry, we may forget to do no harm. We may forget to continue observing patients over time. What impact do the fastest medications have on the rest of the body, and are they skewing other organic functions? Do quick surgical recoveries make athletes more vulnerable to re-injury? Will the abbreviated number of counseling sessions miss the deeper roots of the dilemma?

The demands being made to speed up time ultimately involve dark magic. It serves, instead, to be cautious in our desires to accelerate healing processes. True magic lies in remembering that even Mother Nature has limits. Give her the right amount of time, and we can trust she'll get the job done. Rush her along, and the deep and lasting healing wished for by all involved may not come about.

In our roles, we get to take part in some truly magical moments. Let's not forget that when they happen, powers much greater than us are also at work.

Practices

- Regardless of where they are in the healing journey, ask those in your care what "healing" means to them and what expectations they have in regard to time. Respond to any unrealistic expectations with a version of "Let's both be open to you healing quickly, and this often takes x amount of time."
- Explore how you respond if someone you're tending is healing more slowly than the norm. How might you shift from impatience and blame to responding with compassion?

Plant Seeds

Although we sometimes get to take part in magical moments, much more of our work resembles that of the gardener laboring in the field. We explore with those in our care what combination of sun, soil, nutrients, and water will help them survive and grow to their full potential. Gardening takes time, patience, and regular tending. It requires that we keep our senses open, continuing to watch, listen, and touch as conditions change over time.

As gardeners, the task of planting seeds takes on special importance while working with patients. Along the way, we often offer forms of guidance: exercises to perform, changes in diet, books or websites to explore, classes of interest, homework, and practices to take on. With each of these suggestions, we're planting seeds of change.

Sometimes we're impatient gardeners. We expect that once planted, the seed should bear fruit right away—certainly no longer than a few days or a week! We expect patients to make substantial changes in their thoughts, feelings, or behaviors in very short periods of time. This rush to early ripening creates surplus suffering for all involved.

Dr. Worsley suggested looking in the mirror whenever we're impatient with how long it's taking for a patient to make changes. Looking at the length of time *we've* taken to make substantial changes in our lives is usually enough to give us pause.

In *Earthspirit,* Michael Dowd writes about a kind of date tree that takes eighty years from the time it's planted to bear its first fruit.[3] Eighty years! The person planting the seed most likely will not be around to see the fruits of his or her labor. We can also remember the stoneworkers of past times building the great cathedrals of Europe. They also labored, knowing they wouldn't be around in one hundred years to see the finished structure.

Are we willing to learn from those who planted date trees and built cathedrals? Are we willing to plant seeds day in and day out—even if we won't see them all bear fruit in our time with patients?

We get to be magicians, sometimes catalyzing instant change. More often than not, we guide patients in changes that will take place over time. We learn to trust that the seeds of our actions live well beyond the moment when they're first offered. With the patience and regular tending of skillful

---

[3] Michael Dowd, *Earthspirit: A Handbook for Nurturing an Ecological Christianity.* Twenty-Third Publications, 1991.

gardeners, we commit to creating the conditions in which those we're tending will truly thrive.

Practice

- Introduce the metaphor—planting seeds of change—as a way to describe the first steps those you're tending will take in their healing. Have a conversation about what will support the seeds growing to maturity and bearing the fruit of lasting change.

Part Three
Ways of Speaking

Whether those in our care are experiencing acute trauma, facing chronic illnesses, actively dying, or are committed to strengthening their present states of health, the conversations we create matter a great deal to patients. These conversations are not the sole bailiwick of the physician, psychologist, or social worker; they are human conversations between those giving and receiving care.

Those who've been offering care for a long time deeply understand the power of these conversations. They know that words have power, give power, and take power away. They know that words act like drugs, affecting human biology, physiology, and chemistry. Much more than just air passing over teeth and tongue, they use language to teach, guide, explain, encourage, motivate, inspire, and reassure.

These essays explore ways to use language as medicine. Over time, we learn that conversations with those in our care aren't an accessory to the relationship; they're a critical component of the relationship. With practice, we can train ourselves to skillfully use language in our work. What a joy to discover that the words we use, the conversations we create, the questions we ask, and the stories we tell contribute depth to the healing relationship.

Create Empowering Narratives

There's what's so—and what we say about what's so. There are the phenomena of life and the stories we make up about the phenomena. Those in our care *don't* always have a choice about what happens. They *do* always have a choice about what they say about it.

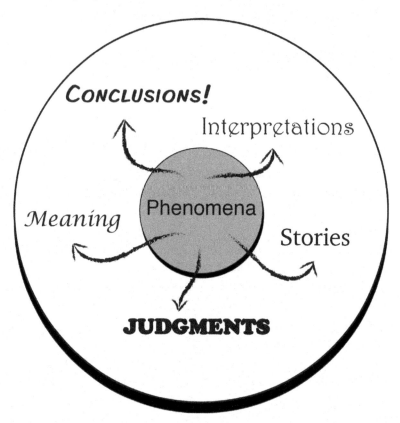

Human beings are pattern-seeking, meaning-making creatures. Making up stories is what we do. The stories and narratives patients create about their circumstances can be a source of surplus suffering or great empowerment.

For example, a man has a heart attack in his midfifties. The stories he could create about that event range from, "Boy, I'm really getting old ... it's all downhill from here," to "That was quite a wake-up call ... it's time to get back in shape." Which stories do you say would be more empowering to this man?

Becoming a Healing Presence

Patients arrive with stories about the past, the present, and the future. Some stories limit, restrict, and restrain them in their journeys back to wellness. Operating out of these limiting stories adds to their pain.

Take a moment to reflect on the following examples. How would you help a patient enlarge and expand these stories?

- "This is only going to get worse."
- "I don't think you'll be able to do much for me."
- "Nothing has worked in the past."
- "I've never been very disciplined."
- "This is really going to be a challenge."

Here are some possibilities of how we might respond:

- "This is only going to get worse."

There's no need to argue here. In fact, sometimes things do get worse before they get better. Let's acknowledge that as one possibility—while creating several other scenarios that point in the direction of improvement.

- "I don't think you'll be able to do much for me."

Again, no need to argue as we don't yet know the full extent of what we'll be able to do together. "How about we get to work and find out what's possible?"

- "Nothing has worked in the past."

"Really, nothing has worked? Not even for a minute? Tell me more about what you've tried and what you noticed along the way."

- "I've never been very disciplined."

I have yet to run into a patient who's not disciplined at something in their lives. Find out what those things are. Help the patient transfer those practices to the situation at hand.

- "This is really going to be a challenge."

Again, this may very well be true. What lies ahead may be the most difficult thing they've ever had to do. At the same time, all patients have faced challenges at some point in their lives. Find out what they were, and how they moved through them. Identify successes from the past—and apply what they did in the past to achieve a successful outcome in the future.

By creating new narratives about their situations, patients engage one of the most powerful healing tools: their imaginations. This increases the number of possibilities of how they might respond to their illnesses.

Facing medical challenges contains enough pain. We can decrease surplus suffering by helping our patients create more enticing and more empowering stories. Healing the story helps heal the patient.

Practices

- Listen closely to the story or narrative that accompanies a patient's description of what's going on. When the narrative is a disempowering one, challenge the patient to create new ones that offer more possibilities. Help the patient move from small mind to large mind in his or her conversations.
- Practice using the word *imagine* in conversations with your patients. In addition to asking them what they think or feel about their situations, ask what they imagine their situations to be. "What do you imagine is going on here?" "What do you imagine lies ahead?" "What do you imagine will get you through this?" You'll find some of the responses to be surprisingly insightful and revealing.

Have Conversations That Matter

I received a phone call from a young man I hadn't seen in several years. He said, "It's important that I come talk to you now."

And talk we did, for about an hour and a half at the end of my workday. He had recently undergone a second surgery to remove cancerous lymph nodes. We never did get to any acupuncture needles, yet he left with several new possibilities for how he might respond and adapt to his current circumstances. Those circumstances included the challenge of how to live in the unknown.

Dianne Connelly said, "There are three things of which we can be relatively certain: we're here, we're here together, and there will come a time when that's no longer so." She added, "What's the conversation worth having in the meantime?" Dianne's question offers us a powerful way to focus on what's important in our conversations with those in our care.

In our desire to truly listen to patients, it's still quite common to find ourselves off track. We sometimes swing to the other end of the pendulum, lending an ear far too long in what I call "dead-end conversations." In addition to their present complaints and concerns, patients sometimes stray into their stories about what others should be doing with their lives, reciting the litany of all they feel is wrong with the world, and what others should be doing to fix it. We can recognize these conversations because they move in circles, often get repeated, and lead to nothing changing.

One effective way to keep patients on track is being aware of what tense the conversation is taking place in: past, present, or future. Conversations about the past do serve a purpose; it's important to hear the patient's story of how they came to this point in time. There also comes a moment when that conversation is complete, meaning any further conversation about the past begins to lose its value. We can bring it to a close by taking a moment to acknowledge all that's taken place and saying, "That certainly sounds like it's been difficult for you. I'm sorry that's been so painful."

The same moment provides an opening to change the conversation to the present tense. What's true for them right now gains importance and value. Skillful inquiry here reveals the unique features of their conditions, steps they're taking to tend themselves, and what changes they're noticing as a result. Sometimes those in our care are already on the mend by the time we see them, and our interventions can be adjusted accordingly.

We then create even more traction for patients by steering the conversation to the future. Whatever the circumstance, the question that again comes to the fore is, "What's possible for you, and how will you go about creating it?" This is the place where we cocreate a step or practice that patients carry out in the interim, amplifying the effect of our time together with them.

Over time, and given the chance, I've found that most people find the future much more compelling than the past. When called to it, they realize the past is the past and what's more important is what lies ahead. How will they adapt to what's taking place, especially if storm clouds are forming on the horizon?

Clearly, these conversations rarely unfold in quite the linear manner just described. Especially when beginning to tell their stories, patients often wander all over the map. The important question remains: are we having the conversations with patients that truly matter to them? When not sure I'm on track, I find myself asking them that very same question.

Conversations we have with those in our care are the heart of the healing relationship. So much so that what we offer in addition—be it a foot massage, an acupuncture needle, herbs, or medication—are really just extensions of the conversation. Engaging our patients in conversations that matter honors the precious time we have with them and brings meaning to the healing relationship.

Practices

- With conversations that tend to stay focused on the past, design simple questions that will shift the conversation to the present or future: "How are things for you today?" "What are you noticing in your body right now?" "What can you be doing this week to improve things for yourself?"
- At the end of each patient visit, write down the rough percentages of time the conversation was spent in the past, present, and future tenses. Do those percentages represent time well spent? If not, make a note to shift the conversation appropriately the next time you see the patient.

Listen for Plastic Words

Some words become so flexible and malleable from common usage, they end up meaning just about anything. The word depressed provides a great example of a plastic word. I've heard it used to describe everything from being upset about missing a workout at the gym to concern over not being able to work sixty hours per week. Similarly, plastic words used by patients include *stressed*, *anxious*, *overwhelmed*, and *burned out*. Truly, I have no idea what these words mean. Do you?

Any named disease—asthma, cancer, heart disease, or diabetes—could be added to our list of plastic words. Doing so is *not* denying that something important is taking place. On the contrary, it calls us to listen even more closely to understand what patients mean when they use these words.

What we listen for is how particular symptoms, signs, and named diseases live uniquely in our patients. To find out more, I sometimes ask new patients to pretend I'm from another planet and have no idea what they're talking about, which is really not that far from the truth! I inquire more deeply about their unique, embodied phenomena. "Where do you feel this?" "When do you feel this?" "How long have you experienced it?" "Where do you notice it in your body?" "What makes it better or worse (temperature, climate, food, time of day, season, exercise, rest, fluids)?" "Please tell me more." "Tell me everything you know about this."

Working within this context, it can be said there is no such thing as asthma, cancer, heart disease, or diabetes. These singular nouns, like most named illnesses, don't all fit a singular clinical picture or result in the same outcomes. An individual's constitution, previous medical history, lifestyle, age, and other factors affect how each is experienced.

Asthma ranges from brief childhood episodes that disappear in time to a chronic, debilitating disease. Cancer shows up as anything from a once-and-done episode with minimal intervention to months and years of treatment and observation. Heart disease and diabetes may respond to simple changes in eating patterns and exercise or require lifelong regulation with medication.

Another factor is the growing body of research confirming that positive attitudes by patients contribute to successful clinical outcomes. These attitudes arise from the stories patients create about their illnesses. Does a particular patient hold cancer as a death sentence or a life-changing wake-up call? Is heart disease perceived as the beginning of the end or the birth of new ways of living? Is the patient creating a narrative of hope and possibility—or one of despair and resignation?

After listening to patients talk about their illnesses, I sometimes ask them to create a second, third, or even fourth story about it. The question then becomes which story provides the most room for them to live and thrive in? Why not choose *that* story to operate out of in the next few weeks or months? When patients realize they have choices about how they speak about their illnesses, they're empowered at a time when they may be feeling quite powerless.

We deepen healing relationships by taking the time to dissolve plastic words and come to know the unique phenomena that patients are experiencing. Equally critical is assisting patients in creating the most empowering stories about their illnesses. Seasoned caregivers share a secret in this regard. They know the real joy lies in tending the patient and not the disease.

Practices

- Question what's unique about how a patient experiences an illness. What's different in how the migraine, the lower back pain, asthma, etc. shows up in them? Finding out what's different or unique often reveals a key piece in how to effectively tend them.
- Find creative ways to guide patients toward more empowering narratives about their illnesses. "What's the title of the next chapter in your book?" "What's in your toolbox that can be pulled out to help you here?" "What does the wise person—the sage or crone in you—have to say about this?"

Help Patients Acknowledge What Is So

Those in our care desire life to be different than it is: to not have this disease or that illness, this pain or that suffering. This desire can be a double-edged sword. For some, their desire will become great sources of motivation in their healing journeys. For others, the same desire crashes head-on with their own resistance and denial. In attempting to face life exactly as it is, they often resist the very steps that may aid them in getting well.

I heard the story about a man who—when presented with the possibility by his physician that he may have celiac disease—said, "I will not give up eating wheat and gluten." Another man I'm acquainted with has known of his highly elevated PSA count for more than a year. During this time, he has refused to have a biopsy of his prostate. What began as prostate cancer has now metastasized to several other parts of his body.

Acknowledging what is so—especially if one has a serious or life-threatening disease—provides everyone involved an opportunity to look at the situation with new eyes and new ears. Resistance and denial often mask fears and reasons why patients don't think they can move forward. A few simple words of acknowledgment bring the conversation back to present tense and can start a new conversation, "I'm sorry you're in pain right now." "I understand this is hard for you." "What else is going on for you today?"

Bowing to life exactly as it is doesn't imply passivity or resignation. We can accept what is so and still be in a conversation about what else can be done under the circumstances. Conversations about possibilities are conversations about hope and action, which is potent medicine indeed.

Practices

- Ask questions of those you tend that guide them to observe what is so in the moment. "What is happening for you now?" "How are you holding up?" "What's helping you bear this?"
- Have conversations that direct patients toward multiple possibilities for how they might move forward in their journeys. "What choices do you have here?" "What else might you do for yourself in the next few weeks?" "What direction do you see yourself moving?"

Make Sure There's No "It" Out There

Hidden in language are subtle but powerful ways in which patients shy away from acknowledging what is so. The word *it* can fall into this category. You've probably heard patients use the word like this:

- "It's really sad."
- "It's really confusing."
- "It's really scary."
- "It's really hard."
- "It's really painful."

With all that's going on with *it*, maybe we should be tending *it* rather than the patient! Using the word in this fashion places the patient in a passive position: a victim of *it*.

Several difficulties arise when using the word *it* this way. First, doing so mistakenly identifies where the *it* (sad, confusing, scared, hard, painful) is located. The difficulty is somehow out there and not perceived as happening in our patient's body. Second, locating the *it* outside the body greatly decreases the patient's ability to shift *it*. They will be less sad, confused, and scared only if *it* changes.

Read these alternatives to see how the focus shifts back to the patient:

- "I'm really sad."
- "I'm really confused."
- "I'm really scared."
- "I'm finding this really hard."
- "I'm in pain."

Calling our patient's attention to this distinction in language takes only a few seconds. Because of this long-standing habit, a number of corrections may be required before a patient appreciates the difference.

Shifting the conversation back to what the patient experiences in his or her body produces big rewards. The patient can then be less the victim of *it* and a more responsible participant in the healing process.

Practice

- Tune your ears to how a patient uses the word *it*. Making light of this distinction the first time you offer it reduces a patient's resistance to changing how they speak. "Sounds like *it* is really having a hard time." "Let's go offer *it* some help!"

Listen for the Opening

In tending those in our care, it often seems there's just no time for any other kind of conversations other than "just the facts." However, when pain, symptoms, and illness continue over an extended period of time, it's fair to assume the roots run deep.

By not having a conversation about these persistent signs, are we allowing them to head toward further illness? In the same vein, if patients are unable to create empowering or meaningful narratives for themselves, does this affect their prognoses? If, through illness, patients lose or forget their purpose in life, could they not be altering the outcomes of treatment for the worse?

Whether layperson, volunteer, or professional, there's always one step we can take: to listen for the moment when there *is* an opening. Not initiating these broader and deeper conversations when the moment presents itself denies our patients a powerful means of healing themselves.

I often use the occasion of the first visit to ask a surprising question, but it instantly deepens the conversation. After taking the time to establish a good level of rapport, I ask, "What are you doing here? Not here in my office on a Thursday afternoon for your appointment—what are you doing here on the planet?" Usually, the patients blink their eyes, snap their heads back a bit, and pause. Most patients identify other human beings as their reason for being on the planet—to share their lives with, to support, and serve their spouses, partners, children, parents, communities, etc.

Two things happen by asking that question. First, it acts as a powerful reminder to patients that they're not only here for themselves. Their health, well-being, and lives matter to others. Second, the question releases a large dose of motivation, courage, and resolve that may be needed for the road ahead.

Treating the branches of an illness without tending the roots doesn't make for effective health care. It's essential to go deeper, especially in the presence of persistent pain and chronic symptoms. Listen for the opening. The conversations that seem like a luxury to us are anything but for those in our care.

Practices

- When you see, hear, or sense an opening for a deeper conversation, take the opportunity to have it. The phrase "Tell me more about …" will open up a new conversation.
- Many patients ask, "What does this all mean going forward? What am I supposed to do now?" Practice folding the questions back on them. "What does this mean for you? What do you want to do now?" Let patients discover for themselves the answers to these questions.

Take Risks

We provide simple, physical comforts to our patients almost without thinking. Whether it's ensuring they're warm enough, providing extra pillows while tending them, or making the smallest pinch when drawing blood, these soothing gestures support the healing relationship.

At times, however, it becomes necessary to disturb our patients' emotional and mental comfort, purposely shaking them up in order to bring them out of the harmful trances into which they've fallen. The kind of risk I'm addressing isn't about changing established protocols or violating accepted standards of care. It's the risk of offending a patient, losing our connection because of what we say.

Over the years, I've told some patients that it's time for them to grow up. I've instructed patients to simply stop what they were doing or saying. I've asked, "What would it be like to never tell that (self-deprecating) story about yourself again?"

Taken out of context, my comments appear rude, arrogant, or presumptuous, and maybe they were all that. However, what I observe happening is that patients rapidly blink their eyes, get red in the face, swallow, and then say something like, "You're right."

I've come to trust the different kinds of knowing within me; I trust that whatever thoughts and feelings *persistently* arise in me in the presence of patients are valuable in tending them. The knowing that comes from my head I call *intellect*. The thoughts arising from facts, data, information, and history are precious indeed! The knowing that comes from my heart I call *intuition*. This felt sense arises in the presence of a heart-to-heart connection. The knowing that comes from my gut I call *instinct*. I feel this deep, primal sensation and awareness of fight, flight, or freeze deep in my belly.

Sometimes our intuitions and instincts are totally on the mark. The conversation takes a valuable turn, the one we're tending has an epiphany, or we receive important information we may not have gotten otherwise.

For example, I once had a conversation with a patient who was an executive of a large company, overseeing hundreds of employees. He had numerous complaints about his current position and the direction in which the company was moving. This ongoing issue was affecting his sleep, eating habits, and exercise routine. My instinct was to challenge him. I took a risk and called his halfhearted efforts to explore the job market "passive." Not a word that executives like to be called!

He returned for only a few subsequent treatments. A short time later, someone close to him told me he had taken a dream job and had moved with his family halfway across the country! I believe my words provoked him in a positive way to take a huge and healthy step forward in his life.

At other times, we will be off the mark. We'll know because our offerings are met with blank stares, rolling of the eyes, or shrugs of the shoulders. Having set a proper context by acknowledging that we were taking a risk, our errant offerings will be quickly forgiven and forgotten.

Intellect, intuition, and instinct share common roots. Each arises from the same practice: being present with patients with senses wide open. We see what's present and that which is hidden. We hear what's spoken and what's left unsaid. We feel the first waves of emotion from our patients and know the currents run much deeper.

Even if we're attentively listening for that opening to a deeper conversation, it may not come. Then it's time to take a risk, buckle ourselves in, sit up straight, and go for it. Those in our care are not as fragile as we think. What we say or inquire about often generates conversations patients have never had before.

Practice

- When a particular thought, feeling, or sensation persists in you in the presence of a patient, bring it up and ask them about it. I often preface my statement or question by saying, "I'm going to take a risk," "I'm not sure what this means," or "This may sound crazy."

Call Patients Back to Wholeness

In the presence of illness, those we're tending often forget *who* they are in their cores and *what* they're capable of in the world. This kind of amnesia shows up as helplessness or powerlessness, feeling they're not up to the task. Some common phrases we hear include:

- "I don't think I can do this."
- "It's going to be really hard."
- "I'm not very good at this."
- "I'm probably going to mess this up."
- "I'm never going to get better."

Whether learning to eat a gluten-free diet, doing physical therapy after surgery, attempting to lower high blood pressure, or recovering from cancer treatments, there will be moments in the journey when those in our care don't believe life will get better.

These are critical moments in the relationship. One person in the room has to *not* conspire with the patient, *not* be infected by their frustrations, and *not* forget what they're capable of—even in the midst of illness. This is an essential task. Holding steady in these moments can be a tipping point in a patient's return to well-being.

I challenge us to operate from the declaration that no matter what has happened, those we're tending are still whole. Everything they need to heal is in them and around them. It requires that we hold our patients as whole and complete—*and* they struggle when eating foods containing gluten. They're not broken—*and* they may have just had surgery. They're not in need of being fixed—*and* they have high blood pressure. Quite a paradox, isn't it?

Those in our care are always more than a collection of symptoms and signs, more than the diagnosis and prognosis, more than the disease. One organ or system not functioning perfectly need not diminish the whole person. We can remind them of the extraordinary human capacities that remain in place—the ability to

- laugh, have fun, and experience joy;
- love and be loved;
- appreciate beauty;
- assert meaning;

- define individual purpose;
- wrestle with truth;
- grasp fleeting bliss;
- glimpse the transcendent; and
- face the mysteries of pain and suffering.

Let's call patients back to wholeness when they forget. Let's make sure there's at least one person in the room holding them as one.

Practices

- How might you respond when someone in your care vocalizes laments as in the phrases above? Practice by writing down several responses you could make to each of the phrases.
- Offer patients reminders of the many human capacities that remain—even in the midst of illness and disease. Take time to reflect and write down some questions that would move the conversation in this direction.

When a Patient Doesn't Know

It's not an uncommon experience for us to ask patients a question and they reply, "I don't know." It could be a simple information-gathering question such as, "When did you first notice *x* happening?" It could also be something more substantial like, "How do you feel about this?" or "What does this mean for you?" In hearing "I don't know," we often conclude we didn't ask the question properly, or we succeeded somehow in confusing our patient. We're quick to repeat the question or ask it again in a different way.

We tend to forget one very effective response on our part: give the patient additional time and space to come up with an answer. Some patients' memories are not the same as they once were; they process information more slowly than they did in the past. Others know what they want to say, yet they struggle to find the words. And still others, especially if we've asked a question of some import, are being drawn deeper into themselves to provide an answer.

Providing our patients time and space in these moments works wonders. It's not that they don't know; it's that they don't know *yet*. We sit back a bit, take a breath, and remain quiet for a moment. Those with sluggish memories have time to catch up, those who struggle with their words end up finding them, and those who've been drawn deeper into themselves realize they do have an answer.

Even when given time, a patient may still say, "I don't know." We could reply, "Imagine or pretend that you do know. What would your response be?" This question is surprisingly effective in evoking a reply.

At other times, patients sincerely don't know. They can't remember in the moment, don't have the words, or are unable to access how they feel inside. We acknowledge their responses and make a note to come back to the question at a later time.

More often than we think, "I don't know" from patients actually means they're close to unearthing something important about themselves. They're standing on the brink of a discovery. The next moment often produces a revelation well worth the wait.

Practices

- The phrase "I don't know" from patients is only one phrase that might warrant a pause on our part. Tune your ears to other phrases that often precede insight and clarity bubbling up in patients:

    - "I'm confused."
    - "I don't understand."
    - "I'm not sure what that means."
    - "I can't figure that out."

- A patient may continue to express that they don't know, are confused, don't understand, etc. Helping them get more specific often opens doors:

    - "Exactly what are you confused about?"
    - "In particular, what don't you understand?"
    - "What are you not sure about specifically?"
    - "What is it really that you can't figure out?"

Tom Balles

When You Don't Know

Whether tending one person all day long or seeing dozens in the course of a day, we're asked many questions by patients and drawn into many conversations. Some of them relate to topics that are outside our knowledge or expertise. Hopefully in these moments we're also able to say the words, "I don't know." The two vignettes that follow point to limits we bump up against—no matter the level of care with which we're involved.

When I first began my acupuncture studies in 1982, there were two books written in English on the topic. Over the past thirty years, the number of translations and new texts has grown exponentially. Even if I tried, I couldn't digest all this new material. Patients ask if I do this technique or that, and I respond that I haven't learned it. How ironic that after thirty years of practice, there may be more I don't know than do know about my own modality of care! The same may be true for many of us: the learning field always stretches well beyond the horizon.

In the eighties, I spoke to a physician in San Francisco. We both were tending a large number of patients who were HIV positive or had AIDS. I was worried that I wasn't learning enough about all the new medical cocktails being developed and their effects on patients. I felt some relief in hearing the physician say that even he couldn't keep up with all the new information rapidly appearing at the time.

The constantly growing learning field and the velocity of change within the field create distinct limits to any of us—layperson, volunteer, or professional. For example, I get asked, "Should I be taking extra calcium?" "I wonder if I should go on an antidepressant?" "Do you think I should be utilizing hormone replacement therapy?" Not being a nutritionist, psychiatrist, or endocrinologist, I don't have the knowledge to respond effectively to these questions. Research over the years has also led to new conclusions in these arenas.

The important distinction is for us to be clear about what we know, what we don't know, *and* to be able to say to those we're tending, "I don't know." What we say carries great weight in the healing relationship, and we're responsible for everything we say while administering care.

How might we respond to questions that are beyond our expertise or scope of practice? We could begin by saying that we don't know. That's closest to the truth. Then we could wait that extra moment to see where they go next in the conversation. We can listen more deeply to discover our patients' true concerns. We can refer them back to their physician for guidance in fields in which we're not competent to speak. We can make referrals to other knowledgeable providers or point them to resource materials that discuss their concerns. We can call patients back to the wisdom of their own bodies—what they are seeing, hearing, or sensing from inside. We can fold the questions back on our patients, asking them what they think they should do.

We're not required to be omniscient. Our care doesn't demand we provide opinions about every medical topic under the sun. At the very least, our attempts to do so jeopardize the relationship with those in our care. In the worst case, we could put our patients' health and our livelihoods at risk.

Those we tend don't expect us to know everything about everything; let's not expect that of ourselves. Maintaining clear boundaries around what we know and what we don't serves everyone in the healing relationship.

Practices

- In addition to saying, "I don't know," practice utilizing some of the other responses noted above: listening more deeply, making referrals, calling patients back to their own bodies' wisdom, and asking patients what they think they should do.
- Take a moment at the end of each day to review the interactions you've had with your patient(s). Note anything you said that puts you close to—or beyond—the boundary of what you know. Make a mental or physical note—or take a similar step that will alter your behavior the next time you're with that person.

Tom Balles

Be as Good as Your Word

Being skillful in performing our tasks is certainly a key factor in being a healing presence. Yet to a degree much greater than we think, trust is also a critical component in providing excellent care. The next two essays explore how to build and maintain that trust by taking distinct actions in language. More on this subject can be found in *Language and the Pursuit of Happiness*[4] by Chalmers Brothers.

Those in our care make requests of us on a daily basis. When we accept and say yes, we're making agreements. Often what happens next is that circumstances and conditions change. The ailing family member being tended at home asks to be woken up for his or her favorite TV show, and we forget to do so. A patient in our unit requests an extra blanket, but there aren't any to be found. We promise to show a patient a new exercise, and then run out of time.

The challenge facing us is not *keeping* all the agreements we make; it's *managing* them. We apologize to the patient at home and take steps to make sure it doesn't happen again. We get back to the patient on the floor to let them know it may be a while before the blanket is on its way. We demonstrate the new exercise first thing in the next session.

Whenever we say, "Yes, we will" and then don't, we erode our patients' trust in us. Over time, our public identity is affected; we begin to be seen as untrustworthy and unreliable.

When it becomes clear we're not going to be able to keep an agreement, it's time to take action: have a conversation, pick up the phone, or send an e-mail. Inform the other party about what's changed. Make a new agreement that meets his or her needs and bring it to a successful completion.

Not a day goes by that we don't make agreements, large and small, with those who we tend. Managing these agreements is an essential skill to possess. Our reputations rest on our skills *and* being found trustworthy in the healing relationship.

---

[4] Chalmers Brothers. *Language and the Pursuit of Happiness.* New Possibilities Press, 2005.

Practices

- Take time at the end of the day to review any agreements you've made along the way. Have any circumstances already changed such that you can't keep any of those agreements? If so, take steps to communicate that to the other party and renegotiate what can be done.
- Review any agreements that any other family members, volunteers, or colleagues have made with you. Are any of these not being honored? If so, have a conversation with that person in order to update the agreement.

Make Clear Requests

In offering care, we operate in a web of relationships that often includes the patient's family members and friends, volunteers, and professionals. This requires that we become skillful in making clear requests and responding clearly to requests made by others. Since we've been making and responding to requests since we were children, this is simple stuff, right? Yet the inability to clearly do so is a large source of confusion, disappointment, and misunderstanding. It's not unlike what happens when we don't manage our agreements: we lose the trust of those around us, and our public identities suffer.

When we make requests of others, there are a few steps we can take to ensure the verbal transaction goes smoothly. First, make sure we have what Chalmers Brothers calls a "committed listener." Making a request of a fellow volunteer while crossing paths in the hallway or asking something of a nurse when he or she is focused on a computer screen are two ways to ensure we don't have someone's full attention. The simple step of facing the other with your body and making sure you have eye contact goes a long way toward being heard.

Secondly, it's helpful when making requests to remember they end in question marks. The phrases, "I would appreciate it if ... I'd really like it if ... wouldn't it be nice if ..." are nice sentiments, but they are not clear requests. They're not likely to get us the outcomes we desire. More direct phrases like, "Can you ... will you ... would you?" go a long way toward getting clear responses in return.

Third, it's especially helpful to offer some context around our requests. Letting listeners know why we're asking something of them leads more often to a shared commitment. Revealing the thinking behind our request builds transparency and partnership in the relationships with those around us. "Can you sit up now so you don't choke while eating dinner?" "Can you get me these forms now since the patient is ready to leave?" "Can you roll over so I can complete this procedure?"

For those in professional roles, it's also critical to understand the difference between making a request of another and making a demand of them. When making a request, the other has the "dignity of decline." Their response of no is okay with us, and it doesn't have any distinct consequences (other than the potential for hurt feelings).

At other times, we do make demands of others around us. Other people can still say no, but by doing so, there will be distinct, and at times, significant consequences for them. A supervisor of volunteers presents a new safety procedure that must be followed, a charge nurse insists that all patient notes be completed before going off shift, or a clinical supervisor demands attendance at the weekly staff meeting. Other people can still say no, but there will be a price to pay for doing so.

It's also important to look at how we respond to requests made of us by patients, coworkers, and colleagues. Sometimes we find ourselves mumbling a response, hemming and hawing, or reluctantly agreeing to a request. An effective alternative is to respond with a crisp and clear yes, no, or by making a counteroffer. These responses greatly reduce the amount of confusion and misunderstandings down the line.

Also helpful in responding to requests is being clear about the time frame of when we'll do what's been asked. Our common responses of "pretty soon ... when I get a chance ... later on" are equally vague and may lead to unnecessary disappointment on the part of the other.

Effective communication is the lifeblood of relationships with all those involved in patient care. By making clear requests and responding clearly to the requests of others, we keep those lines of communication open. Misunderstandings are kept to a minimum, and we maintain our reputations as reliable and trustworthy providers of care.

Practices

- Tune your ears to when requests are being made of you, even if they don't end with a question mark. Is it clear what's being requested (i.e. who's to do what by when)? Respond clearly to those requests by offering a simple yes, no, or counteroffer.
- Underneath many squawks and complaints are unspoken requests. Listen for the request hidden beneath the squawk, and follow up with a question that will help reveal it, as in the following examples:

    - "It's really cold in here."
    "Would you like me to get you another blanket?

    - "I'm really getting confused."
    "Would you like me to go over the directions again?"

    - "I don't like taking all these medications."
    "Shall we review them and see if we can make any changes?"

Tom Balles

Hold Symptoms and Signs as Wise Teachers

If only our bodies could speak to us in our native tongues! If only they could leave a phone message, send a text or e-mail, all would be well. In fact, our bodies do speak to us all day long. The challenge is being aware of these messages and determining how best to interpret them.

Symptoms and signs are teachers, guides, and allies in the healing process. They're the equivalent of the phone message, text, or e-mail; something wants our attention.

Years ago, a woman came seeking acupuncture treatment for frequent headaches. Looming large for her was the challenging relationship with her domineering husband. She was angry at the whole situation. In the presence of frequent headaches, our first inclination might be to somehow quiet the headaches and help the patient "resolve" them in some fashion. She did receive some relief with her headaches, yet they persisted.

Over a period of time, she came to realize that her husband and living situation weren't the source of her anger or her headaches. Something deeper inside was longing to come forth: the dream of being an artist. She took the huge step of enrolling in a fine arts school in another city. Doing so required renting a small apartment so she could stay there several days a week. Over time, her headaches diminished. Though unpleasant, they had been an ally in her journey—letting us both know that something inside her still hadn't been tended.

It's absolutely true that a headache can just be a headache, and a backache can just be a backache. They can be temporary blips on the screen. The symptoms and signs that persist, however, tend to be messages from deeper parts of the human psyche. Our bodies and flesh are the medium via which messages get conveyed.

How sad that in our contemporary Western world, the many aches, pains, and suffering of life have all somehow become medical problems to be fixed. The primary measure of success has become the ability to make pain and suffering, signs and symptoms disappear. Within this world, it becomes a radical notion to hold symptoms and illnesses as potential friends. It definitely takes some getting used to. My headaches are an ally? Absolutely! Menstrual cramps are my guide? Yes! Lower back pain is my teacher? Of course!

Our bodies do speak. They constantly convey wisdom to us. They know what they need, know how to heal themselves, and sometimes need assistance from others in doing so. Let's encourage those we tend to observe their bodies, listen to them, feel what's going on inside, and speak about the messages they're receiving. In accepting patients' bodies as wise teachers, we become the humble students. What better way to learn how to tend those in our care?

Practices

- Introduce your patients to the notion of symptoms and signs as wise teachers and guides rather than phenomena to make disappear. What can be learned from them to aid in healing?
- Rather than directly asking, "How are your headaches, menses, backaches, etc.?" practice asking patients what new messages they're receiving from their bodies since they've last seen you. This question guides patients to become better observers of their bodies.

Go Beyond the Literal

Sometimes our bodies do speak in words. With a little practice, we can tune our ears to hear them.

Past experiences that gave birth to guilt and shame, the deeper painful wounds received from others, our internal conflicts, and challenges to our identity are never quite as hidden as we think. The unfinished business speaks to us via symptoms and signs; it also speaks through the language used by those in our care.

As you read the expressions below, ask yourself these questions: Are these just random, well-worn phrases that patients coincidentally happen to use? Or are they very distinct, revealing figures of speech for what's actually happening deep inside the patient? If we blur the line a bit between the figurative and the literal, might we discover a powerful way for patients to return to well-being?

- "It's like I got punched in the gut."
- "It's a thorn in my side."
- "It's like a knife through my heart."
- "It's a pain in the ass."
- "I got knocked over by the whole thing."
- "I'm drowning in this."
- "I'm feeling smothered."
- "I can't stomach this anymore.'"
- "It's gut wrenching."
- "It burns me up."
- "My blood is boiling."
- "It was shocking."
- "I'm in pieces."
- "It's too much to bear."
- "I'm really feeling drained."
- "It's making me sick."
- "It's killing me."

Whole new conversations open up when we encourage patients to think about the figures of speech they're using. Simple questions spark their imaginations, and patients begin to see they can take actions to heal themselves.

- "How does one recover from being punched in the gut?"
- "How will you take that thorn out of your side?"
- "What can you do to prevent yourself from drowning?"
- "How does one recover after being shocked?"
- "How will you go about picking up the pieces?"

We speak in figures of speech all the time—they express what lies underneath waking consciousness.[5] With practice, a few questions from us allow those we tend to give voice to the unspoken, make the invisible visible, and put in our patient's hands that which has been out of their reach.

Practices

- Make it a practice to write down one figure of speech you hear from every patient you see. Initially, you might think this a difficult task. Trust me—once you start listening for them, you'll hear them everywhere.
- As a way to begin, when patients offer up clinical labels for what ails them—insomnia, migraines, chronic fatigue syndrome, etc.—ask the simple question, "What is that like?" Patients will often have an expression on the tips of their tongues that you can work with to find new responses to their situations.

---

[5] This essay is but the tip of the iceberg of how one can work with patients' figures of speech. A deep bow to Andrew T. Austin for his ongoing work in developing ways of relating to patients and their language. I highly recommend his training called "Metaphors of Movement" and his book, *The Rainbow Machine*. For more information, visit http://metaphorsofmovement.co.uk

Tom Balles

Stay until the End

Some years ago, I was tending a man with AIDS who would be the third of three sons in the same family to die from the disease. He was clearly weakening, yet his death did not appear imminent.

I treated him at home one day and asked what he wanted. He said he wanted clarity in making a decision. I needled two acupuncture points with the beautiful names of *Bright and Clear* and *One Hundred Meetings*. The next day, he went to the hospital for some routine tests, felt too fatigued to come home, and died there the next day. I believe the treatment helped him clarify his thinking, and he decided it was time to let go.

It seems harsh to write that all those in our care are dying; yet it's true. Each day we're alive brings us closer to the end. For some of our patients, death is not imminent; for some, it is. This leads us to ask, how does the healing relationship change when it's clear that a patient is actively dying?

The simplest answer is that we continue offering the many gifts outlined in these essays. Let's choose to keep our senses open and stay present to the sights, sounds, and smells that accompany the dying process. We can remember to breathe, stay centered in ourselves, and listen to our patients' concerns. We make room for ambivalence and face the myriad emotions arising in our patients (and ourselves) as they face the end. Let's allow ourselves to be moved by the mystery that is life and death. Let's remember that toward the end, the quality of our being matters more than what we are doing.

Our time with the dying need not be filled with conversation. Sharing quiet time together or simply bearing witness to what is happening in the moment can be a precious gift to both the giver and receiver of care. The offering of physical touch is another special gift that's often well received—even by patients who were not previously comfortable with touch. I remember how my dying father's eyes would roll upward with delight as his adult children took turns massaging his hands, feet, arms, and legs. I dare say all of us enjoyed more physical contact with him in those final weeks than we had in previous times.

The patients' recognition that these are the final days often (but not always) produces many positive transformations and healing. Estranged relationships can and do get reconciled. Patients' temperaments and personalities can change for the better. Letting go of life provides the opportunity to let go of all the old stories that no longer serve. Much healing can take place at the same time our patients are dying.

I'd like to say that tending dying patients gets easier as we gain more experience. Given the uniqueness of each patient and his or her situation, I'm not sure this is true. A patient approaching death is one place in the healing relationship where both parties find themselves beginners. Let's allow for some stumbling and fumbling on everyone's part, and let's accept that awkward conversations are not uncommon.

I do know that staying till the end seasons us as providers of care. We discover courage and humility within ourselves that can't be obtained any other way.

Practices

- Make room for dying and death to take many different forms. Stay open to healing taking place even in the very last moments. Choose to stay present with your patient. Stay until the end.

Final Thoughts

The practices outlined in these essays constitute a powerful form of self-medication. They'll ward off any impending amnesia we face and remind us of what truly matters when offering care:

- that we offer our unique gifts as human beings and cultivate ourselves as instruments of healing
- that we remember our great capacity to help heal other human beings
- that we not lose the healing power of the relationship between those giving and receiving care

In the coming decades our life spans will continue to lengthen, and we'll see an increase in the aging population. There's already a growing need for those who offer care—laypersons, volunteers, and professionals alike.

To meet this great need, it's essential that we have the support of personal and professional communities around us. We'll need to stay in conversations with family members, friends, and peers about the ongoing challenges we face. None of us can do this work alone.

Offering care over the past thirty years has been an extraordinary privilege for me, and I hope you find it to be the same for you. Our ways of being, doing, and speaking touch and influence everyone around us, including our patients. Knowing that, let's bring open hearts, open minds, and open hands to all those in our care.

Further Reading

Achtenberg, Jeanne. *Imagery in Healing Shamanism and Modern Medicine.* Boston: Shambhala Publications Inc., 1985.

Acosta, Judith and Judith Simon Prager. *The Worst Is Over.* San Diego: Jodere Group, 2002.

Andreas, Steve. *Transforming Negative Self-Talk.* New York: W.W. Norton & Company, 2012.

Austin, Andrew T. *The Rainbow Machine.* Boulder: Real People Press, 2007.

Balles, Tom. *Dancing with the Ten Thousand Things Ways to Become a Powerful Healing Presence.* Lincoln, Nebraska: iUniverse, 2004.

Balles, Tom. *Cultivating a Healing Presence*, a guide.

Brothers, Chalmers. *Language and the Pursuit of Happiness.* Naples, Florida: New Possibilities Press, 2005.

Carson, Shawn and Melissa Tiers. *Keeping the Brain in Mind.* New York: Changing Mind Publishing, 2014.

Connelly, Dianne M. *All Sickness Is Home Sickness.* Columbia, Maryland: Traditional Acupuncture Institute, 1986.

Connelly, Dianne M. *Medicine Words.* Laurel, Maryland: Tai Sophia Press, 2009.

Duggan, Robert M. *Common Sense for the Healing Arts.* Laurel, Maryland: Tai Sophia Press, 2004.

Duggan, Robert M. *Breaking the Iron Triangle: Reducing Health Care Costs in Corporate America.* Columbia, MD: Wisdom Well Press, 2012.

Flores, Fernando. *Conversations for Action and Collected Essays.* North Charleston, South Carolina: CreateSpace Independent Publishing Platform, 2012.

Frank, Jerome D. and Julia B. *Persuasion and Healing.* Baltimore, Maryland: The Johns Hopkins University Press, 1991.

Harris, Sam. *Free Will.* New York: Free Press, 2012.

Hillman, James. *Healing Fiction*. Woodstock, Connecticut: Spring Publications, 1983.

Illich, Ivan. *Limits to Medicine Medical Nemesis: The Expropriation of Health*. London: Marion Boyers Publishing, 1976.

Loy, David R. *The World Is Made of Stories*. Somerville, Massachusetts: Wisdom Books, 2010.

McNeilly, Robert B. *Healing the Whole Person*. New York: John Wiley & Sons, 2000.

Mercier, David G. *A Beautiful Medicine*. Easton, Maryland: Still Pond Press, 2012.

O'Hanlon, Bill, Sandy Beadle. *A Guide to Possibility Land*. New York: W.W. Norton & Co., 1997.

Poerksen, Uwe. *Plastic Words*. Translated by Jutta Mason and David Cayley. University Park, Pennsylvania: Pennsylvania State University Press, 1995.

Prager, Judith Simon. *Journey to Alternity*. Lincoln, Nebraska: Writer's Club Press, 2000.

Prochaska, James O., John C. Norcross and Carlo C. DiClemente. *Changing for Good*. New York: HarperCollins Publishers, 1994.

Rollnick, Stephen, Willliam R. Miller, Christopher C. Butler. *Motivational Interviewing in Health Care Helping Patients Change Behavior*. New York: The Guilford Press, 2008.

Schwartz, David B. *Who Cares? Rediscovering Community*. Boulder, Colorado: Westview Press, 1997.

Senge, Peter, C. Otto Scharmer, Joseph Jaworski, Betty Sue Flowers. *Presence*. Cambridge, Massachusetts: Sol, 2004.

Sieler, Alan. *Coaching to the Human Soul*. Victoria, Australia: Newfield, Australia, 2003.

Smith, Fritz. *Inner Bridges*. Atlanta: Humanics New Age, 1986.

Smith, Fritz. *The Alchemy of Touch*. Taos, New Mexico: Complementary Medicine Press, 2005.

Sullivan, John. *The Spiral of the Seasons: Welcoming the Gifts of Later Life*. Chapel Hill, North Carolina: Second Journey, 2009.

Sullivan, John. *Living Large Transformative Work at the Intersection of Ethics and Spirituality*. Laurel, Maryland: Tai Sophia Press, 2004.

Thomson, Garner and Khalid Khan, *Magic in Practice*. London: Hammersmith Press, 2008.

Tiers, Melissa. *Integrative Hypnosis*. New York: Melissa Tiers, 2010.

Watzlawick, Paul. *The Language of Change.* New York: W.W. Norton & Co., 1978.

Zander, Rosamund Stone and Benjamin. *The Art of Possibility.* Boston: Harvard Business School Press, 2000.

Ziegler, Alfred J. *Archetypal Medicine.* Woodstock, CT: Spring Publications, 1983.

About the Author

Tom Balles has been a practicing acupuncturist for three decades. He holds a Licentiate in Acupuncture (LAc) from the College of Traditional Acupuncture, Royal Leamington Spa, UK, and a master's degree in acupuncture (MAc) from Tai Sophia Institute.

Tom has been teaching in the graduate degree programs at Tai Sophia Institute (now Maryland University of Integrative Health) since 1996. He also served two terms as Dean of Faculty of the acupuncture program. Through selection by graduating students, he is a five-time recipient of the Great Esteem Award in recognition of his outstanding commitment and contribution to students' learning and excellence as practitioners.

Tom is also the author of *Dancing with the Ten Thousand Things: Ways to Become a Powerful Healing Presence* and *Cultivating a Healing Presence*, a guide.

He lives and practices acupuncture, Zero Balancing®, and Integrative Hypnosis in Laurel, Maryland. Tom can be reached through his website: www.tomballes.com.

For more information on certificate and degree programs at Maryland University of Integrative Health: www.muih.edu.